MW01093025

Boy Scouts of America
WILDERNESS
First Aid Manual

Boy Scouts of America
WILDERNESS
First Aid Manual

Buck Tilton, MS, WEMT
Foreword by William W. Forgey, MD

FALCONGUIDES

GUILFORD, CONNECTICUT
HELENA, MONTANA

AN IMPRINT OF GLOBE PEQUOT PRESS

FSC

Mixed Sources
Product group from well-managed
forests, controlled sources and
recycled wood or fibre

Cert no. SCS-COC-002464
www.fsc.org
© 1996 Forest Stewardship Council

FALCON GUIDES

Copyright © 2010 by Boy Scouts of America
Supplemental material © 2010 by Buck Tilton

FalconGuides is an imprint of Globe Pequot Press.

Falcon, FalconGuides, and Outfit Your Mind are registered trademarks of Morris Book
Publishing, LLC.

Illustrations by David Gross, Judy Newhouse, and Robert Prince

Project editor: Jessica Haberman
Layout artist: Melissa Evarts
Text design: Sheryl P. Kober

Library of Congress Cataloging-in-Publication Data is available on file.

ISBN 978-0-7627-5949-1

Printed in the United States of America

10 9 8 7 6 5 4 3 2 1

The author and publisher have made every effort to ensure the accuracy of
the information in this book at press time. However, they cannot accept any
responsibility for any loss, injury, or inconvenience resulting from the use of
information contained in this guide. Readers are encouraged to seek medical help whenever possible. This book is no substitute for a doctor's advice.

CONTENTS

FOREWORD

Recognizing the lack of a national standard for wilderness first aid, the Boy Scouts of America formed a task force consisting of wilderness medicine specialists, medical epidemiologists, legal experts, and educators to develop a curriculum and doctrine for a 16-hour wilderness first aid (WFA) course. Buck Tilton was the lead author of this project. As author he had to amalgamate the results of the literature research performed by the task force and oversee multiple revisions until this final product was developed. The task force is indebted to Buck for his hours of dedication to the project.

Persons taking this course will have an appreciation of how wilderness first aid differs from standard, urban first aid. Many readers will want to learn more about this fascinating and critical skill needed by all outdoor travelers. Some will be inspired to continue their education with a wilderness first responder course.

This book contains the full doctrine that the task force approved. It provides a portable resource for use in the field as well as a text for the WFA course. It will be your introduction to the basic skills and knowledge all wilderness travelers should possess.

—*William W. Forgey, MD*
BSA Wilderness First Aid Task Force Chair

ACKNOWLEDGMENTS

More than any other book I have written, and, in the truest sense of the words, this work is the result of a team effort. The team leader was William W. "Doc" Forgey, MD. One of my greatest privileges has been to work with Doc Forgey on this and numerous other projects. Also sharing Doc's vision and commitment, was Ruth Reynolds, RN, the Boy Scouts of America (BSA) medical coordinator. It was a great honor and pleasure to work with her and the rest of the members of the BSA Wilderness First Aid Task Force. And so, many thanks to The Force:

Christine Cashel, EdD
Charles (Reb) Gregg, Esq.
Jeffrey L. Pellegrino, PhD
Arthur (Tony) Islas, MD
Loren Greenway, PhD

Richard Bourlon
Lindsay Oaksmith
Richard M. Vigness, MD
Jennifer Surich

And the Consultants:

David Bell, PhD
Pat Noack

Sven Rundman III
Brad L. Bennett, PhD

INTRODUCTION

Wilderness first aid (WFA) is the assessment of and treatment given to an ill or injured person in a remote environment where definitive care of a physician and/or rapid transport is not readily available. Time, therefore, is the essential element distinguishing wilderness first aid from standard first aid. When definitive care is far away, the principles of standard first aid are often unequal to the task of managing the injured and the ill. Consider also the rough trail, the wandering length of river, or the long miles of black asphalt separating the patient from a medical facility. Think about the heat or cold, the rain, the wind, the darkness. Remember that equipment needed for treatment and evacuation may have to be improvised from what is available, and communication with the "outside world" may be limited or nonexistent. Remote locations and harsh environments may require creative treatments. All these things are the stuff of wilderness first aid.

This book resulted from the need for a text for a standard wilderness first aid course. This wilderness first aid curriculum was developed by a task force formed at the invitation of the Boy Scouts of America. Its mission was to specifically write the curriculum and the associated doctrine guidelines that describe what should be taught in the course. The small book you hold covers all the information described by the Boy Scouts of America Wilderness First Aid Curriculum and Doctrine Guidelines (WFACDG), currently available online at www.scouting.org. Supplemental material is included that is *not* described by the WFACDG, and all such material is clearly shaded to distinguish it from the WFACDG.

It is the responsibility of those who play, work, and live in isolated places to be able to act appropriately in an emergency. Wilderness first aid skills can be learned, and though excellent opportunities to gain the necessary knowledge and practical skills were few and far between not long ago, now they are available regularly in many communities.

As a prerequisite for the BSA WFA Course, you must be currently certified in cardiopulmonary resuscitation (CPR) and use of an automated external defibrillator (AED). This book assumes the reader has such training.

Note: This book does not pretend to have all the answers. It provides principles for dealing with many serious emergencies and a few common problems. It is intended to be a reminder about what to do for those who have training and a stimulus to learn for those who are untrained. It is not intended to be a substitute for professional medical care when such care is available.

ACTION CHECKLIST

- ☐ Take a deep breath. Stay calm. Take charge. Be quick but not hasty. Act fast—but go slow.
- ☐ Before stepping in, assess the situation and make sure the scene is safe.
- ☐ Perform an initial assessment, treating the patient for any immediate threats to life or limb.
- ☐ Perform a focused assessment, examining the patient for problems and gathering information.
- ☐ Sit down, take a deep breath, look around, and plan what to do. Treatment must be considered and carried out, an evacuation may need to be prepared, help may need to be requested.
- ☐ Stay or go, fast or slow? If an evacuation of the patient is necessary, decide if you need to move quickly or at a more leisurely pace.
- ☐ Keep a written record of the emergency. Be ready to give a verbal report.
- ☐ Act in the best interest of the most people.

1.
PATIENT ASSESSMENT

GENERAL INFORMATION

Patient is the term used to describe the person to whom you will be giving first aid. Before you can properly care for any patient, you have to assess what is wrong with the person. An assessment is a step-by-step process. Although some of the steps may change in order, depending on the immediate status of the patient, no step should be left out.

ESTABLISH CONTROL

Emergencies, small or large, may be charged with emotion and confusion. Even minor chaos increases the risk of injury to rescuers and bystanders and the risk of inadequate care for the patient. Emergencies most often call for a leader to be directive, at least until the scene is safe and the patient is stabilized. This is best accomplished by discussing leadership in case of an emergency with other members of your party *before* a potentially critical situation occurs.

In an emergency, two qualities in a leader are necessary. The first is competence. That means you know your stuff; you are capable and ready to act. The second is confidence. You appear able to deal with the situation. You don't have to *feel* confident, but you should *appear* confident and *sound* confident. Avoid shouting. Speak with quiet authority, and then listen. Your goals should be to first provide the greatest good for the greatest number in the shortest time, and secondly to do no harm.

ASSESS THE SCENE

Before rushing to a patient's side, take a few moments to stand apart and assess the scene, checking for specific information.

1. Make sure the immediate environment is safe. Is there immediate danger to you, other rescuers, bystanders and/or the patient(s)? You must do all you can to ensure you never create an additional patient. Humans, among other things, are resources. Additional patients not only double the trouble but also reduce the resources; the problem becomes more than twice as serious.
2. Establish body substance isolation (BSI). Take precautions— put on non-latex gloves and/or glasses (such as sunglasses), for instance—to protect you and the patient from germ transmission.
3. Determine, if possible, the mechanism of injury (MOI) based on your immediate observations. Are there clues suggesting what happened to the patient or the forces involved in the patient's injury? How far, for instance, did a patient fall, and what did he or she land on?

PERFORM AN INITIAL (PRIMARY) ASSESSMENT: ABCDE

Once safely at your patient's side, perform an initial assessment. The goal is to identify and treat any immediate threats to life. If you discover a threat, stop and fix it. Immediate loss of life will be from ABCDE: A) loss of an **A**irway; B) inadequate or nonexistent **B**reathing; C) loss of adequate **C**irculation because the heart has stopped or too much of the patient's blood is leaving the circulatory system (e.g., onto the ground or spilling inside a body cavity); D) extensive **D**isability from damage to the spinal cord; or E) extremes of the **E**nvironment. (**E** also reminds you of your need to **E**xpose injuries or possible injuries in order to assess them.) You will be asking questions.

1. Identify yourself and your level of training, and ask for consent to provide care: "Hi, my name is _____ and I've been trained in wilderness first aid. Can I help you?" If the patient says something like "Yes" or nods in acceptance, or even says nothing to indicate lack of consent, you have consent to treat.

2. Control the patient and gather information. Say something like "Please, do not move until I know more about you. Can you tell me who you are and what happened?" The patient may identify a chief complaint, saying something such as "I twisted my knee, and it really hurts." If the patient does not identify a chief complaint, ask the patient what he or she thinks is wrong. If the information you gather leads you to

suspect a possible spine injury, place a hand on the patient's head and remind the patient to remain still.

Note: A patient who cannot respond requires your immediate CPR training.

3. Assess using the ABCDE method.
   (A) Check the patient's **a**irway. A patient who is speaking has an open airway, but ask if he or she has any problem breathing.
   (B) Assess **b**reathing. If breathing is difficult, you need to figure out why and fix the problem. This book addresses some breathing problems that were not covered in your CPR course.
   (C) Assess **c**irculation. Check for a pulse at the wrist on the thumb side. This book addresses some things you can do for a pulse that is too fast or too slow. Then perform a quick scan for major bleeding. You may need to check, with your gloved hand, inside bulky clothing and/or underneath patients who are lying on a surface, such as snow or fallen leaves, that can hide bleeding. If you find bleeding, immediately expose the wound and use direct pressure to control the bleeding. This book addresses other methods of controlling bleeding.
   (D) Assess for **d**isability. If you suspect a spine injury, keep a hand on the patient's head or ask someone else to take control of the head. This book addresses spinal injuries.

(E) Assess the threat of the **e**nvironment and **e**xpose injuries. Prolonged exposure to environmental extremes can cause changes in body core temperature that may threaten the patient's life. The most common threat is cold. To avoid changes in body core temperature, a patient should be protected from the environment. If the threat is not extreme, protection may wait until you know more. If necessary, you must sometimes expose parts of the patient's body at skin level in order to assess the extent of damage and provide immediate care.

PERFORM A FOCUSED (SECONDARY) ASSESSMENT

When the patient is free from all immediate threats to life, you need to start gathering clues. The focused assessment, a focused exam and history, continues the step-by-step examination of the patient. The goal is to find everything that is not in perfect working order. Since these problems are not immediate threats to life, treatment can usually wait. This examination includes three phases:

Hands-On Physical Exam

Check the patient from head to toe to locate any damaged parts. Look for wounds, swelling, or other deformities. Ask where it hurts and if it hurts when touched. Feel gently but firmly, using a massage-like action with your hands spread wide to elicit a pain response but without causing further damage. Be aware of unusual smells (e.g., alcohol) or sounds (e.g., labored breathing). If you suspect an injury may be hidden beneath clothing, you must take a look at skin level. "Go to skin to assess" is the mantra of the rescuer.

Check:

1. **Head,** looking for depressions in the skull, damage to the eyes, and fluid in the ears, nose, or mouth.
2. **Neck,** pressing on both sides for pain or deformity.

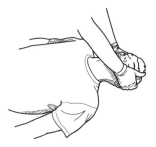

Check Head

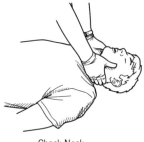

Check Neck

3. **Shoulders,** for pain and symmetry of the shoulders, including the clavicles (collarbones).

4. **Chest,** for pain, ability to take a deep breath, uneven breathing movements of the chest wall, and abnormal breathing sounds. Press on both sides of the chest and ask the patient to take a deep breath. Press on the sternum as a separate check.

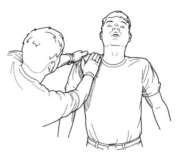

Check Shoulders

Check Chest High and Low

5. **Abdomen,** gently pressing on all four quadrants (with the belly button as the central point) for pain.
6. **Pelvis,** for pain by pushing both in and down on the two pelvic crests.
7. **Genitals,** if and only if it seems relevant.

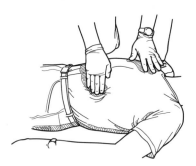

Check Abdomen All Four Quadrants

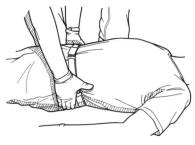

Check Pelvis

8. **Legs,** for pain and including symmetry and the ability to move the feet. With both hands, squeeze the legs circumferentially as you move down their entire length.

9. **Arms,** for pain and including symmetry and the ability to move the hands. With both hands, squeeze the arms circumferentially as you move down their entire length.

10. **Back,** After this head-to-toe check, roll the patient flat on her or his back to assess the back. If the patient has an injury that could have damaged the spine, the roll must be performed carefully (see Spine Injuries). Press on every bone of the spine. *Note:* This is a fine time to place the patient on a pad as protection from the cold ground.

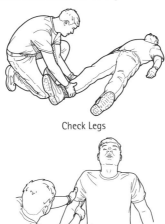

Check Legs

Check Arms

Vital Signs

Vital signs are measurements of the physiological processes necessary for normal functioning. They do not often tell you what is wrong, but they do tell you how the patient is doing. Changes in vital signs over time are indicators of changes in the condition of your patient. Check early, and keep checking. To better monitor a patient, record the time at which you take each set of vitals.

Vital signs include:

Level of Responsiveness (LOR)

The level of responsiveness is a check on how well the brain is communicating with the world. Use the AVPU scale for quick reference.

(A) Is the patient **a**lert and able to answer questions?

    A+Ox4: Patient knows who, where, when, and what happened.

    A+Ox3: Patient knows who, where, and when.

    A+Ox2: Patient can only relate who and where.

    A+Ox1: Patient only remembers who she or he is.

(V) Does the patient respond only to **v**erbal stimuli, by grimacing or rolling away, for instance, from your voice when you speak or shout? In what way does she or he respond?

(P) Does she or he respond only to **p**ainful stimuli, such as a pinch? In what way does the patient respond?

(U) Is she or he **u**nresponsive to any stimuli?

Heart Rate (HR)

The heart rate is a check on how well the heart is pumping blood to the rest of the body. Count the number of heartbeats per minute by pressing two or three fingers just above the wrist on the thumb side where you find the radial pulse. For speed, count for 15 seconds and multiply by four. Note the rhythm and quality of the pulse. Is it regular or irregular, weak or strong? Normal heart rates are strong and regular and usually somewhere between 50 and 100 beats per minute.

Respiratory Rate (RR)

The respiratory rate is a check on how well the patient is breathing. Count the number of breaths per minute without telling the patient what you are doing. A patient who knows you are checking often alters the breathing rate in an attempt to be accommodating. Note also the rhythm and quality of respirations. Normal lungs work about 12 to 20 times per minute at a regular and unlabored pace.

Note: Without a watch, you should still get a rough estimate of heart and respiratory rates. Rough guesses are better than no idea.

Skin Color, Temperature, and Moisture (SCTM)

The condition of the skin reflects how well the patient's brain, heart, and lungs are functioning. Normal skin is pink in non-pigmented areas (such as the inner surface of the lips and eyelids), warm, and apparently dry to your touch. Normal skin, therefore, is pink, warm, and dry. Note alterations from normal that may appear, for example, as pale, cool, and damp or red, hot, and dry.

Take a SAMPLE History

More information is usually gathered by subjective questioning than by objective checking. This information is known as a patient's history. Hopefully the patient will provide the answers. Sometimes witnesses are sources of important information. Speak calmly, and do not use leading questions. In other words, say "Describe your pain" instead of "Is it a sharp pain?" Be aware of your tone of voice, body language, and eye contact. Patients usually feel better and respond better if they think you are nice— but do not make promises you cannot keep. If you gain trust, you must maintain trust.

The SAMPLE Questions:

(S) Ask the patient about his or her symptoms. Is the patient experiencing any pain, nausea, lightheadedness, or other things you can't see?

(A) Ask the patient about his or her allergies. Are there any known allergic reactions? What happens? Has there been any recent exposure to an allergy-causing agent?

(M) Ask the patient about any medications he or she might be taking. Are they over-the-counter? Prescription? Why is it taken? When was it last taken?

(P) Ask the patient for any pertinent medical history. Has anything like this happened before? Is the patient currently under a physician's care for anything?

(L) Ask the patient about his or her last intake and output: When was food or drink last taken? How much? When were the most recent urination and defecation? Were they normal?

(E) Ask the patient about the events leading up to the accident or illness. What led up to the events? Why did it happen?

DOCUMENT THE INCIDENT

The acronym SOAP reminds you to write everything down as soon as possible on your report form—as long as taking notes does not interfere with patient care. Retention of information for medical and legal reasons is important.

(S) Find out about the subjective information. Who (age and gender) is the patient? What are his or her complaints? What happened?

(O) Obtain the objective information, including the results of the patient exam, vital signs, and SAMPLE history.

(A) Assess the patient. What do you think is wrong?

(P) Plan your treatment. What are you going to do immediately for the patient? Answer the evacuation question—stay or go, fast or slow? A part of every plan is to *monitor* the patient for changes and developing needs.

SAMPLE VERBAL SOAP REPORT

If you can make radio or phone contact and ask for support, you will need to give the SOAP note in verbal form. The person hearing your verbal SOAP should hear something like this:

(S) I have a 23-year-old male patient whose chief complaint is right knee pain. The patient states, "I was running and stepped in a hole and twisted my right knee."

(O) The patient was found lying on his back about 3 miles from Lander on the Middle Fork Trail. Patient exam revealed swelling of the right knee. The right knee is about twice the size of the left knee and red in color. Patient denies loss of consciousness. Patient denies pain or tenderness along the spine. There is normal circulation below the right knee. Nothing else was found.

At 3:00 p.m. the vital signs were LOR=A+Ox4; HR=78 regular and strong; RR=18 regular and unlabored; SCTM=pink, warm, and sweaty.

The patient reported the following history: No symptoms other than pain in the right knee. Patient is allergic to aspirin but denies taking aspirin. Patient denies taking any medications. Patient denies pertinent medical history. Patient describes his fluid intake as "about 2 quarts of water today" and his food intake as "two ham and cheese sandwiches" for lunch. He reports a clear urination "about an hour ago." Patient states he was not watching the trail closely and failed to see the hole.

(A) Based on the MOI this is not a possible spinal injury. His problem is a right knee injury that makes walking impossible.

(P) I will improvise a splint for the right knee. I am alone, and I will need a litter and assistance to carry the patient to the trailhead.

2.
CHEST INJURIES

GENERAL INFORMATION

Any significant injury to the chest may lead to difficulty breathing, a potentially serious and life-threatening problem. You must be able to properly identify and provide first aid for all chest injuries, recognize when a chest injury is serious, and know when and how fast you need assistance.

GUIDELINES FOR ASSESSMENT AND TREATMENT

Injuries to the chest may involve the bones (ribs and/or clavicle), the lungs, or both.

Bone Injury

Pain is present with a rib or clavicle (collarbone) injury, and the patient usually complains of an increase in pain when a deep breath is taken. There may be discoloration (bruising) where the bone is broken. You may notice some swelling. The patient often guards the injury, protecting it from being moved or touched. If, however, you gently touch along the bone, you will usually find a point (sometimes called "point tenderness") where the pain is most intense.

A simple fractured rib or clavicle can be protected by supporting the arm on the injured side with a sling-and-swathe. Take care to construct a sling-and-swathe that supports the weight of the arm on the injured side (see Bone and Joint Injuries). Do *not* wrap a band snugly around the patient's chest. Do encourage the patient regularly to take deep breaths, even if it hurts, to keep the lungs clear of fluid, particularly if an evacuation will be lengthy. A simple fractured rib or clavicle does not require an immediate evacuation, but a patient assessed as having a fractured bone does need to be evaluated by a physician. Be sure to monitor the patient for increasing difficulty breathing.

Lung Injury

A simple fractured rib will not be so simple if a bone fragment punctures a lung. Air escaping the lung and collecting in the chest is called a *pneumothorax*. A patient with a pneumothorax often has increasing difficulty breathing and a rising level of anxiety. A pneumothorax can worsen until the patient is unable to breathe adequately, a condition known as a *tension pneumothorax*, which may result in death. Suspicion of a pneumothorax calls for an immediate evacuation. There is no other first aid treatment available at the wilderness first aid level other than treatment for a fractured rib.

If several ribs are broken in several places, a free-floating section of chest wall, called a *flail*, may result. A flail will involve injury to the lung beneath the flail. The flail will move in opposition to the rest of the chest wall during breathing. Flails are not common, but when they occur it is a life-threatening situation that requires evacuation. The speed at which this is done can make the difference between life and death. Note that rescue breathing for the patient may be needed during the evacuation. As an immediate measure to manage the condition, taping a bulky dressing over the flail may allow the patient to breathe a little easier. The tape should not be placed entirely around the chest because this technique will make it more difficult for the patient to breathe. Evacuation of the patient on his or her side, injured side down, sometimes aids breathing.

If the chest has been opened by a penetrating object, the hole may bubble and make noise when the patient breathes. This is called a *sucking chest wound* (*open pneumothorax*), and the hole should be immediately covered with an occlusive dressing—something that lets no air or water pass through. Clean plastic will work. Tape this dressing down securely on all four sides.

Occlusive Dressing on Chest Wound

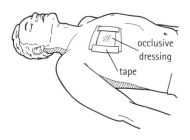

occlusive
dressing

tape

Severe difficulty breathing indicates a tension pneumothorax could be developing; remove the plastic in hopes the trapped air in the chest will be released. If that does not work, consider gently pushing a gloved finger into the hole in hopes of releasing the trapped air. This treatment may be the difference in saving the patient's life. Once again, a speedy evacuation is critical.

HYPERVENTILATION SYNDROME

Not all breathing problems are serious. Pain, fear, and other stresses, for instance, can cause a person to breathe faster and deeper than normal. This hyperventilation syndrome may lead to chest tightness; tingling or numbness in the hands, feet, and/or face; and muscular spasms in the hands and feet—that lead to more fear, that lead to increased hyperventilation. Strongly encourage the patient to calm down and control breathing. The patient that does not calm down may pass out, and breathing may stop for what seems like a very long time. Except in rare cases, the patient will start breathing again. If a minute or so passes without breathing, you can give the patient a few rescue breaths. When normal breathing returns, you can investigate the cause of the hyperventilation.

GUIDELINES FOR EVACUATION

Evacuate—you can go slow—any patient with a suspected fractured rib. Often, a patient with this injury is able to walk. Evacuate rapidly—go fast—any patient who has sustained a chest injury associated with increasing difficulty breathing. In this circumstance, the patient will need to be transported.

3.
SHOCK

GENERAL INFORMATION

Shock is inadequate perfusion, a condition that results when the cardiovascular system is challenged, causing the patient's brain and other body cells to receive a less than sufficient flow of oxygenated blood. It can occur from a great variety of injuries and illnesses including but not limited to: loss of the needed level of fluid in the body via blood loss or dehydration; failure of the heart to pump adequately due to heart attack; or loss of adequate pressure in the blood vessels of the body due to spinal cord damage or a severe allergic reaction. Whatever the cause, shock patients tend to share similar signs and symptoms, and you must be able to intervene with proper care and know when the patient needs a higher level of care than you can provide.

GUIDELINES FOR ASSESSMENT AND TREATMENT OF SHOCK

Patients in shock progress through stages as they deteriorate.
    In the early stages, look for:
1. Level of responsiveness (LOR) that is anxious, restless and/ or disoriented.
2. Heart rate (HR) that is rapid and weak.

3. Respiratory rate (RR) that is rapid and shallow.
4. Skin color, temperature, and moisture (SCTM) that is pale, cool, and clammy (but may be pink and warm in some cases, such as if the shock is the result of an allergic reaction).
5. Symptoms that include nausea (and sometimes vomiting), dizziness, and thirst.

In the later stages, look for:
1. LOR that continually decreases with eventual unresponsiveness.
2. HR in which the radial pulse (the pulse at the wrist) grows increasingly rapid, weakens, and eventually disappears.

Since shock can kill, and since what you can do for shock is limited in the wilderness, early recognition and management are critical.
1. Treat shock early, before serious signs and symptoms develop.
2. If a cause can be identified, such as bleeding or dehydration, treat the cause immediately.
3. Keep the patient calm and reassured.
4. Keep the patient lying down (as found in most cases).
5. Elevate the patient's feet comfortably and approximately 10 to 12 inches. (Injuries to the head or lower extremities may preclude this.)
6. Protect the patient from loss of body heat.

7. Sips of cool water may be given to prevent dehydration
    with shock from any cause if the patient tolerates fluids,
    and his or her mental status allows holding and drinking
    from a container.

Shock Treatment Position

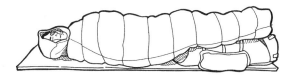

GUIDELINES FOR ASSESSMENT
AND TREATMENT OF HEART ATTACK

Heart attacks (damage or death of part of the heart muscle due to
lack of adequate perfusion) is the leading cause of deaths in the
United States. A heart attack may, but not always, lead to shock.
Not only does shock make the situation more serious—it is often
fatal. What you do, therefore, is of critical importance.

Patients may complain of center-chest discomfort such as
crushing, squeezing pain, or heavy pressure. Pain, predominantly
on the left side, may radiate to the shoulder, down the arm, or
into the jaw. Nausea, sweating, and shortness of breath are common. Patients often deny the possibility that this could be a heart
attack.

In all situations, you need to:

Keep the patient physically and emotionally calm, in a position of comfort (usually *not* lying down), and warm. Do not allow the patient to walk, even short distances. Call for help.

In the wilderness, you should:

Give the patient four 81-milligram aspirins or one 325-milligram aspirin. If the patient has been prescribed nitroglycerin, one pill should be placed under the tongue with the patient sitting—but only if the patient has a strong radial pulse. Most physicians recommend a second pill after 10 minutes if the first fails to work and a third after another 10 minutes if the second fails to work.

GUIDELINES FOR EVACUATION

Evacuate—you can go slow—any patient with early signs and symptoms of shock that do not stabilize or improve over time. Evacuate rapidly—go fast—any patient with decreased mental status or worsening vital signs, especially if the patient's heart rate keeps speeding up. Go fast if your assessment is heart attack. All of these patients will need to be carried.

4.
HEAD (BRAIN) INJURIES

GENERAL INFORMATION

Anyone who has received a significant blow to the head or face runs the risk of bleeding and swelling of the brain. Because there is little room inside the head for swelling to occur, brain injuries can cause death in a relatively short period of time.

GUIDELINES FOR ASSESSMENT AND TREATMENT

Despite the possibility of heavy bleeding from a scalp wound or the growth of a goose egg–sized bump, a serious threat to the patient is rare if the skull is intact and the brain is relatively undamaged. With a mild head injury, there will be very short-term loss of consciousness or no loss at all. Symptoms may include short-term amnesia, briefly blurred vision, nausea, headache, dizziness, and/or lethargy (abnormal drowsiness or sluggishness). Treat wounds appropriately: Apply pressure from a bulky dressing on the bleeding scalp and a cold pack for the bump. Monitor the patient for about 24 hours. Awaken the patient every 2 hours during the night to check for signs and symptoms of serious brain damage.

A period of unconsciousness during which the patient does not respond to aggressive stimulation should be considered long-term unconsciousness and may indicate serious brain damage.

The injury may or may not involve a skull fracture, which should always be considered severe.

Signs of a skull fracture include:

1. A depression in the skull.
2. A fracture visible where the scalp has been torn revealing the fracture.
3. Bruising around both eyes (raccoon eyes) or behind both ears (Battle's Sign).
4. Cerebrospinal fluid (clear fluid) and/or blood weeping from nose or ears.

Without an obvious skull fracture, patients may at first appear to have recovered but later may start to deteriorate. With or without evidence of a skull fracture, you must watch for signs and symptoms of brain injury. Those signs and symptoms include:

1. Mental status deterioration—from disoriented, to irritable, to combative, to coma.
2. Personality changes.
3. Loss of coordination and/or speech.
4. Debilitating headache.
5. Visual disturbances.
6. Seizures.
7. Persistent nausea and vomiting.
8. Relapse into unconsciousness.
9. In later stages, heart rate may slow and bound, respiratory rate may become erratic, and pupils may become unequal.

If there is an obvious head injury, consider the possibility of a cervical spine (neck) injury. Specific measures to implement during evacuation include the critically important step of establishing and maintaining an airway in all unconscious patients. You can usually keep an airway open by keeping the patient in a stable side position (the HAINES position—High Arm IN Endangered Spine). Alternatively, with consideration for possible spinal injury, place the patient with his or her head elevated approximately 6 to 8 inches.

HAINES Position

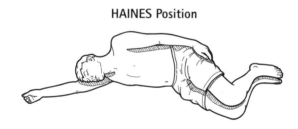

GUIDELINES FOR PREVENTION

Adequate care for a brain injury is not possible in the wilderness. Prevention should rank high among your priorities. In addition to approaching activities safely, wearing a helmet approved for specific activities such as biking and climbing is a must. The helmet must fit the user and be held in place with a non-stretching chinstrap. Wearing a helmet does not eliminate the chance of a serious injury, but it does reduce the risk.

HEADACHES

Headache is a very common and seldom serious complaint. Generally speaking, there are three causes: dehydration, muscular tension, and a vascular disorder. Most headaches improve with some combination of rest, hydration, massage (of the shoulders and scalp), and over-the-counter pain reducers, such as ibuprofen. But beware of the unusual headache that comes on suddenly, that is unrelieved by rest, hydration, and medication, and that is described by the patient as pain unlike any other he or she has experienced. Unusual headaches are reasons to find a doctor.

GUIDELINES FOR EVACUATION

Evacuate any patient who does not respond initially to aggressive attempts at stimulation after a blow to the head. When responsive, this person can walk out if there are no indications of serious head injury. Evacuate rapidly—go fast—any patient with signs and symptoms of severe head injury, especially a skull fracture and/or a decrease in mental status. Serious patients require carrying.

5.
SPINE INJURIES

GENERAL INFORMATION

Damage to the spinal cord may result in permanent paralysis or death. The spinal cord (a bundle of nerves) runs within and is protected by the spinal column of bone. Injury to the bones may not always lead to nerve damage, but it is an indicator that spinal precautions should be taken. For that reason, proper management of a patient with suspected damage to the spinal column is critical to prevent spinal cord damage (if it hasn't occurred already). In the initial assessment, any patient who has a mechanism for a spine injury, especially a cervical injury, should be kept still with your hands on his or her head and calming words said until secondary treatment can be applied.

Note: A patient found unconscious should be considered a spine-injured patient until proven otherwise.

   Highly suspect mechanisms of injury include:
1. Compression/axial loading, such as falling from a height or landing on the head.
2. Excessive flexion, as when the chin is forced to the chest.

3. Excessive extension or rotation, such as tumbling downhill without skis releasing.
4. Distraction, such as an attempted hanging.
5. Penetration, as from a gunshot or stabbing in the area of the spine.
6. Sudden and violent deceleration.

GUIDELINES FOR ASSESSMENT AND TREATMENT

Signs and symptoms of spinal column injury include spine pain, spine tenderness to touch, and obvious injury to the spinal column.

Signs and symptoms of spinal cord injury include:
1. Altered sensations in the extremities such as numbness, tingling, or unusual hot or cold sensations; unusual weakness in the extremities; the inability to move.
2. Respiratory difficulty.
3. Loss of bowel control.
4. Signs and symptoms of shock.

Patients on their back can be log-rolled onto their side to assess the back for injuries. Manual stabilization of the head and neck is critical during the roll. At the command of the head-holder, the patient is rolled *as a unit,* keeping the neck and back in line. Patients must be held stable during the check and rolled back with the same precautions.

Manual Stabilization of Head and Neck

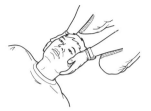

Log-Roll

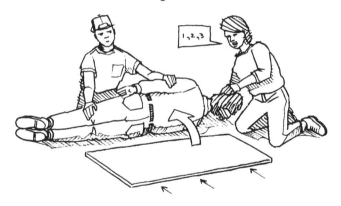

Note: A log-roll can also be used to roll a patient onto her or his side in order to place a pad underneath before rolling the patient back onto the pad.

Patients can also be rolled from side to back and from face down to back using the same precautions. Although it is possible for one rescuer to perform such rolls, two or three rescuers make the job easier and safer for the patient.

If the patient's neck lies at an odd angle, it may be straightened with slow, gentle movement—performed by the rescuer—to line it up with the rest of the spine. This straightening improves the airway and makes immobilization easier. If this movement causes pain or meets resistance, stop and immobilize the patient's head as it lies.

A patient with a possible spinal injury who is found crumpled into an odd body position may be straightened with slow, gentle movement of one body part at a time. This typically makes the patient more comfortable and provides for better immobilization.

When the spine-injured patient has to be moved, such as into a tent for warmth, move her or him via **b**ody **e**levation **a**nd **m**ovement (BEAM). A BEAM requires a sufficient number of rescuers kneeling on both sides of the patient and another rescuer holding the head. The rescuers on the sides gently push their hands underneath the patient. At the command of the head-holder, lift the patient *as a unit* with as little spine movement as possible, and carefully carry him or her, using shuffling steps, to a pre-designated spot. The patient is then lowered via commands from the head-holder.

BEAM

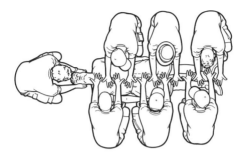

a. Check where hand placement will be.

b. Slide hands beneath patient.

c. On command of head-holder, lift and move.

With the spine in normal alignment, the next step is to restrict spine motion with a cervical collar. Ambulances carry rigid cervical collars. You can improvise one in the wilderness by rolling extra clothing, such as a long-sleeved fleece sweater, or by cutting off the end of a foam sleeping pad to fit the patient's neck and taping it in place. A collar goes completely around the patient's neck. If an improvised collar varies in thickness, the thickest part should be placed between the chin and chest.

Improvised Cervical Collar

Collars, even commercial products, cannot totally stabilize the cervical spine. Hands-on attention should still be maintained, if possible, until the whole patient is stabilized in a rigid litter. In the wilderness, you're often looking at a long wait for a litter, but attempting to move a spine-injured patient without one creates great risk and is *not* recommended. When a litter is available, the patient should be FOAMed in place—made **free of any**

movement—with an adequate amount of padding and straps. Fill any voids with pads under the knees, in the small of the back, and anywhere there's space that could let the patient shift. The patient's head should always be strapped down last. Proceed with care.

FOCUSED SPINE ASSESSMENT

After completing a full assessment on a patient with a mechanism for spinal injury, and after finding no signs and symptoms of spinal injury, you may choose to perform a focused spine assessment in hopes of discontinuing spinal immobilization. A focused spine assessment includes a second check for:

1.   A fully reliable patient. A fully reliable patient is at least A+Ox3 on the AVPU scale, sober and without distractions such as severely painful injuries or deep psychological distress.

2.   A patient without altered sensations in the extremities, such as tingling, or the ability to move the extremities.

3.   A patient with grip strength and the ability to lift the legs against resistance.

4.   A patient who denies spinal pain and tenderness to palpation of the spine.

Note: If in doubt, maintain spinal precautions.

GUIDELINES FOR PREVENTION

In addition to approaching activities safely in general, avoid climbing without safety ropes, diving headfirst into water, riding in a vehicle without seat belts fastened, and skiing with bindings that do not release under the appropriate pressure.

GUIDELINES FOR EVACUATION

Evacuate any patient being treated for a possible spinal injury. Evacuate rapidly—go fast—any patient with the signs and symptoms of spinal cord injury. And remember you will need the assistance of a team—ground or airborne—with a rigid litter.

6.
BONE AND JOINT INJURIES

GENERAL INFORMATION

Injuries to the musculoskeletal system—bones, ligaments, muscles, tendons, and cartilage—are among the most common in wilderness activities. You will often be unsuccessful in your attempt to assess exactly what is wrong, but you need to know how to handle these emergencies.

GUIDELINES FOR ASSESSMENT
AND TREATMENT OF STRAINS

Strains are overstretched muscles and/or the tendons that attach muscles to bones. They can range from a mild annoyance to debilitating. They are indicated by pain and sometimes by bruising in the area of the strain. A strain can be used within the limits of pain—in other words, tell the patient if it hurts, do *not* do it. RICE can be helpful (see Sprains on page 39).

GUIDELINES FOR ASSESSMENT
AND TREATMENT OF SPRAINS

Sprains are injuries to ligaments, the bands holding bones to bones at joints, and can vary from simple overstretching to complete

LOW BACK STRAIN

If a strain involves low back pain and comes on suddenly, apply cold for 20 to 30 minutes, several times a day, for the first 48 hours. If the pain grew gradually, heat usually works best. After 2 days, heat is usually best in both cases. Patient should rest in a side position or on the back with high padding beneath the knees. Massages may help. Reasons to evacuate a back-strained patient include:

1. The pain (or numbness) begins to radiate into the hip and/or thigh or all the way down a leg.
2. The pain remains strong even when the injured area is at rest.
3. The pain started as a result of illness.
4. The pain came on sharply after a fall from a height or a sudden jolting stop.

tears. They are indicated by pain, pain on movement, swelling, and bruising, although bruising may take hours to appear. Unlike fractures that mend strong and strains that heal well, a sprain may come back to haunt you the rest of your life, especially if you treat it improperly. What is really unfortunate about sprains is that they do not hurt as much as they should. Pain would encourage sensible action. Sensible action involves proper first aid and adequate support for the injury.

Note: Strains and sprains, especially where a joint is involved, are often impossible to differentiate. Differentiation, however, is not required. They are treated the same.

First aid is RICE: **r**est, **i**ce, **c**ompression, and **e**levation. But RICE should be applied after an initial evaluation of the injury. The primary goal of the evaluation is to determine if the injury is usable or not. Get the patient at rest and relaxed—and take a look at the injury. Look for deformities, rapid swelling, and discoloration. Have the patient actively move the joint and evaluate the amount of pain involved. Move the joint more aggressively with your hands and evaluate the pain response. Finally, if the joint appears usable, have the patient test it with his or her body weight. A usable injury can be, well, used. An unusable injury will require a splint (see page 43).

Whether the injury is usable or unusable, have the patient stay off the injury (R) for the first half hour while you reduce its temperature with ice (I) as much as possible without freezing the skin. Crushed ice works best. It conforms to the shape of the anatomy involved. Do not put ice directly on skin—put it in a plastic bag and wrap it in a shirt or sock. If ice is not available, soak the injury in cold water, use a chemical cold pack, or (during warmer months) wrap the joint in wet cotton and let evaporation cool the damaged area. Compression (C) requires an elastic wrap. Wrap the elastic snugly but not tightly enough to cut off healthy circulation, and wrap from below the injury toward the heart. Elevation (E) refers to keeping the injury higher than the patient's heart. After 20 to 30 minutes of RICE, remove the treatment and let the joint warm naturally for 10 to 15 minutes before use. *Note:* The injury will heal faster if RICE is repeated three to four times a day until pain and swelling subside.

Ankle Compressed with Elastic Wrap

RICE

(R) **R**est the injured area. Have the patient avoid movement, after your initial evaluation, that causes pain.

(I) **I**ce the injured area. Applying ice or another form of cold can help reduce swelling and ease pain.

(C) **C**ompress the injury with an elastic wrap to further reduce swelling.

(E) **E**levate the injured area above heart level to reduce swelling. Serious injuries to the limbs may preclude this.

Support for Sprains

Usable upper extremity sprains do not typically require support. With usable knee sprains, the patient may be aided by creating a walking splint—a splint that restricts the movement of the knee without putting pressure on the kneecap—for the knee. A pad should be placed behind the knee within the splint to keep the knee slightly flexed. The patient will be further supported by using a stick or staff for balance. Patients with usable ankles should have their boots laced firmly and will also benefit from a stick or staff for balance.

Walking Knee Splint

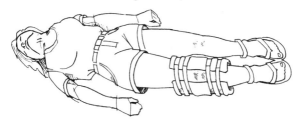

GUIDELINES FOR ASSESSMENT AND TREATMENT OF FRACTURES

Sometimes the assessment of a fracture, a broken bone, is simple: bones stick out through the skin, or angulations occur where no angulation should exist. Without the obvious, and without an X-ray, rescuers can base an assessment on specific guidelines. The goal, once again, is to determine whether or not the injury is usable.

Remove clothing carefully, and take a look at the site of the injury. Is there discoloration and swelling? Does the patient move the injury easily or guard it, preventing motion? Compare the injured side to the uninjured side. Does it *look* broken?

Ask the patient: How did the injury occur? (High-speed impacts cause more damage than low-speed impacts.) Do you think it is broken? (The patient is often correct in his or her assessment.) How bad does it hurt? (Surrounding muscle spasms create pain and give evidence of the seriousness of the injury.)

Gently touch the damaged area. Does the patient react to your touch? Does it feel like the muscles are spasming? Does it feel unstable? Is there point tenderness—one particular spot that hurts noticeably more when touched? These are indications of a fracture.

Check for CSM—**c**irculation, **s**ensation and **m**otion—beyond the site of the injury. Loss of a pulse, numbness, tingling, and inability to move are signs of loss of normal blood flow and loss of normal nerve messages—serious complications with a fracture. After splinting, check CSM often to assure circulation is not cut off by wraps that are too tight.

Note: Patients will usually benefit from RICE, whether the bone is broken or not.

Splinting

The general rule is *When in doubt, splint!* A splint should restrict movement of the broken bone(s), prevent further injury, and maximize patient comfort until a medical facility can be reached. To do this best, a splint needs to be made of something to pad the injury comfortably and something rigid enough to provide support. Padding should fill all the spaces within the system to prevent movement of the injury. In addition, a splint should be long enough to restrict the movement of the joints above and below a broken bone, or restrict the movement of the bones above and below an injured joint.

Splints should hold the injury in the position of function or as close to position of function as possible. Functional positions include:

1. Spine, including neck and pelvis, straight with padding in the small of the back.
2. Legs almost straight with padding behind the knees for slight flexion.
3. Feet at 90 degrees to legs.
4. Arms flexed to cross the heart.
5. Hands in a functional curve with padding in the palms.

In choosing materials for splinting, you are only limited by imagination: sleeping bags, Foamlite pads (and they can be cut to fit the problem), extra clothing, and soft debris from the forest floor stuffed into extra clothing can all serve as splints. For rigidity, there are items such as sticks, tent poles, ski poles, ice axes, lightweight camping chairs, and internal and external pack frames. Lightweight commercial splints are available as additions to your first aid kit. Splints can be secured in place with things like bandannas, strips of clothing, pack straps, belts, and rope. Useful items in your first aid kit for securing splints include tape, elastic wraps, and roll gauze. Large triangular bandages are helpful in creating sling-and-swathes.

Steps to Splinting
1. Assess CSM below the injury.
2. Pad the injury circumferentially.
3. Position and secure the rigid support.
4. Re-assess CSM below the injury.

Specific Fractures

Jaw fractures can be held in place with a wide wrap that goes around the head. Be sure the wrap can be removed quickly if the patient feels like vomiting.

Jaw Splint

Collarbone (clavicle) fractures can be secured with a sling-and-swathe. Slings can be made from triangular bandages or improvised. You can improvise by lifting the tail of the patient's shirt up over the arm on the injured side and safety-pinning it in place. Be sure the sling lifts the elbow to take pressure off the shoulder.

Sling–and–Swathe

Shirt as a Sling

Lower arm (radius and/or ulna) fractures (including wrist and hand) can be secured to a well-padded, rigid support, and then held in a sling-and-swathe. Place a roll of something soft in the hand to keep it in position of function. Secure the hand to the splint to prevent hand movement. If bones of the hand are damaged, be sure to pad the hand well.

Lower Arm Splint

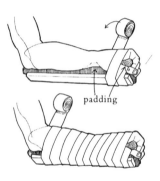

Fingers that are broken can be secured to nearby healthy fingers with padding between them.

Upper arm (humerus) fractures can be placed in a sling-and-swathe. Leaving the elbow free sometimes eases the pain. Secure the broken bone to the patient's chest wall with a wide soft wrap.

Rib fractures can be protected by supporting the arm on the injured side with a sling-and-swathe. Do not wrap a band snugly around the patient's chest. Do encourage the patient regularly to take deep breaths, even if it hurts, to keep the lungs clear. Be sure to watch the patient for increasing difficulty breathing.

Pelvis and hip fractures should include securing the entire patient on a rigid litter before attempting a carry-out. A conforming wrap around the pelvis will provide some support and security for a fractured pelvis, and it should be applied soon after a pelvic fracture is assessed. The conforming wrap need only be 4 to 5 inches wide. Secure the legs comfortably to each other for fractures of both pelvis and hip. Be sure to watch the patient for signs of shock due to internal bleeding common with pelvic fractures.

Leg (femur, tibia and/or fibula) fractures (including the ankle and foot) can be secured with a well-padded, rigid support that

Securing Legs Together

includes immobilization of the ankle and foot. Sleeping pads and lightweight camping chairs can make excellent leg splints. Pad behind the knee for comfort.

Leg Splint

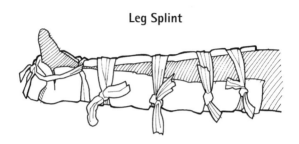

Complicated Fractures

An *angulated fracture* (angles in bones) needs to be straightened. Pull gentle traction on the broken bone *along the line in which it lies.* This relaxes the muscles and reduces the pain, allowing you to move the broken bone slowly and gently back into normal alignment. The sooner this movement takes place the better. Do not use force. Do not continue if the patient complains of increasing pain. Once aligned, splint as usual. If alignment cannot be achieved, splint as best you can.

An *open fracture* is indicated by an open wound at the point of fracture. Bones may or may not be visible. The wound should be irrigated and dressed appropriately, and the bone should be splinted. If bone ends stick out of the wound, and if the doctor is more than 4 to 6 hours away:

1. Clean the wound and bone ends without touching them.
2. Apply gentle traction in line to the fracture and pull the bone ends back under the skin.
3. Dress the wound.
4. Splint the fracture. Infection is on the way, but bones survive better if pulled back inside the body.

GUIDELINES FOR ASSESSMENT AND TREATMENT OF DISLOCATIONS

With a dislocation, the bone ends in a joint are no longer properly aligned. The patient typically experiences pain in the joint and a loss of normal range of motion. The joint will look wrong. Many dislocations can only be managed in the field on a wilderness first aid level by splinting in the most comfortable position. With some dislocations, a field reduction (realignment) may be attempted.

Work quickly but calmly. Typically, the sooner a reduction is attempted, the easier it is on patient and rescuer. Encourage the patient to relax as much as possible, with special concentration on relaxing the injured joint. Reduction may cause pain, but stop if pain increases dramatically. Once reduced, the injury should be splinted.

Specific Reducible Dislocations

Anterior shoulder dislocations are one of the most common. There are several ways to reduce a dislocated shoulder. With the Stimson technique there is little chance of harm to the patient, although it takes time and sometimes fails to work:

1. Position the patient prone (face down) across a rock or log with the arm on the injured side dangling down vertically.
2. With a soft cloth, tie something that weighs about 5 to 10 pounds to the dangling wrist.
3. Wait. This process takes 20 to 30 minutes to work. The key to success is for the patient to be relaxed and to allow the gentle pull of the weight to slowly fatigue the chest and back muscles, thus allowing the head of the humerus to slip along the chest wall and then snap back up into position in the shoulder joint (glenoid fossa). Too much weight will cause increased spasm and prevent this method from working.

Stimson Technique

Persons experiencing a shoulder dislocation can frequently pull the shoulder back into place, if they perform virtually the same maneuver immediately upon themselves. Standing or sitting the patient should pull the injured arm straight forward away from the body by gripping the wrist with the opposite hand. This is the same mechanical maneuver that the Stimson technique employs. If the patient delays more than a few minutes in attempting this reduction, the dislocation will cause so much spasm in the chest muscles that this technique will probably not work.

Upon reducing the shoulder, the patient should be placed in a sling-and-swathe. Do not swathe the patient if the person may need to use the arm in an emergency, such as escaping from an overturned raft or preventing a fall. While it is best that the shoulder be immobilized, allow the patient the ability to use the arm in an emergency.

Finger dislocations are also common. Keeping the injured finger partially flexed, pull on the end while gently pressing the dislocated joint back into place with your other thumb. Tape the injured finger to a neighbor with a gauze pad between them. Do not tape directly over the joint itself.

Kneecap (patella) dislocations are typically very easy to reduce. Apply gentle traction to the leg to straighten it out. Sometimes the kneecap pops back into place when the leg is straightened. If it does not, massage the thigh and push the kneecap gently with your hand back into normal alignment. With a splint that does not put pressure on the kneecap, the patient may be able to walk out.

Toe dislocations are treated similarly as finger dislocations. Keeping the injured toe partially flexed, pull on the end while gently pressing the dislocated joint back into place with your other thumb. Tape the injured toe to a neighbor with a gauze pad between them. Do not tape directly over the joint itself.

GUIDELINES FOR PREVENTION

Attention to safety prevents many injuries. Adequate and properly fitted footwear decreases the chance of injury. Pre-trip physical conditioning prior to wilderness activities may decrease the chance of injury.

GUIDELINES FOR EVACUATION

With a usable injury, the degree of discomfort of the patient will determine more than anything the need to evacuate the patient. Evacuate any patients with unusable injuries and with first-time dislocations (except perhaps dislocations of the outer joints of the fingers and toes). Evacuate rapidly—go fast—any patients with angulated fractures; open fractures; fractures of the pelvis, hip, or femur (thigh); and injuries that create a decrease in CSM beyond the injury.

7.
WOUNDS AND WOUND INFECTION

GENERAL INFORMATION

Wounds, burns, and problems related to the ears, nose, and teeth are among the most common ailments dealt with by all providers of first aid. For the best results for the patient, all wounds should be considered and treated as contaminated. Goals of management include stopping serious blood loss, cleaning wounds and keeping them clean, and treating wounds in order to increase comfort and promote healing.

Note: Use non-latex gloves when there is any possibility of exposure to blood or other body fluids.

Care for the wounds inflicted by the bites of mosquitoes, ticks, and venomous snakes, and treatment specific to those bites, may also be required of the wilderness first aid provider.

GUIDELINES FOR TREATMENT OF BLEEDING

Life-threatening arterial bleeding spurts from a wound each time the patient's heart beats. Venous bleeding, which can also be serious, flows smoothly and rapidly. A quick visual scan of the patient is often enough to detect serious bleeding—but not always! Check inside the clothing of someone wearing bulky winter gear or rain gear. Check beneath someone who is lying in sand, rocks, snow, or any other terrain that might disguise blood loss.

Note: Severe blood loss can also be internal, so monitor for shock.

Almost all bleeding can be stopped with direct pressure, usually applied with pressure from your hand directly on the wound with a barrier between you and the wound. If there is time, place a sterile dressing on the wound before applying pressure. If there is no time, grab anything absorbent to press into the wound. In cases of severe bleeding, packing a wound initially with your fingers, then switching to and packing with absorbent material, can supplement continued direct pressure and may be necessary.

Be aware that some wounds should not be treated with direct pressure. Pressure to a wound on a patient's neck may cut off the air supply. Instead, stop the bleeding by carefully pinching the opening closed. Pressure to a head wound may push cracked bone fragments into the patient's brain. Cover the wound with a bulky dressing and press lightly instead.

If blood loss is tremendous and death imminent, a tourniquet can be used on an arm or leg. Tie a band of soft material, about 4 inches wide, around the limb, approximately 2 inches above the wound. Do *not* use anything narrow, such as a rope or string, as a tourniquet. Tie a short stick or another rigid object into the material to create a windlass technique, and twist it, tightening the tourniquet until bleeding stops—and no more. But it is critically important to check the pulse beyond the tourniquet after application. If you can find a pulse, the tourniquet is *not* tight enough and should be tightened more. Note the time when you apply the tourniquet. These arterial tourniquets are rarely necessary, but if one is required to control bleeding, apply and keep it on continuously until the patient reaches definitive surgical care. In a very remote area where care might not be reached for days, continuous application will result in loss of the limb. Only in this situation will it be appropriate to release the tourniquet approximately every 2 hours while continuing to apply direct wound pressure, in order to assess the continued need for the tourniquet and to diminish the possibility of distal limb loss. If bleeding has remarkably slowed or stopped, replace the tourniquet with a pressure dressing. If bleeding remains persistent, replace the tourniquet. It is more important to save a life than a limb. Assessment of continued bleeding can be accomplished within 1 second of release. In all situations, it is better to apply a tourniquet prior to seeing the signs and symptoms of shock (see Shock). If there has been extensive blood loss, and the person is already in shock or it is difficult to assess the amount of continued bleeding, leave the tourniquet in position and *do not* remove it. Continuous tourniquet application is preferred to allowing additional blood loss.

Tourniquet

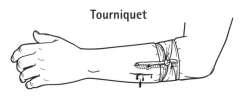

GUIDELINES FOR ASSESSMENT
AND TREATMENT OF SOME WOUNDS

Abrasions are shallow and often dirty wounds that occur when some skin has been scraped away. If treated within approximately 10 minutes, abrasions can be treated by simply applying a thick layer of antibiotic ointment and covering it with a sterile dressing. If treated later, abrasions should be scrubbed clean. You can scrub with a gauze pad or a clean, soft cloth. With gauze or pad, clean with soap and potable water. Follow scrubbing with irrigation or rinsing. Apply a thin layer of antibiotic ointment, then a dressing and bandage.

Lacerations are cuts through the skin that have either even or ragged edges. They will vary in depth. Skin around a laceration should be washed clean prior to thorough irrigation of the wound. There is no definitive amount of water to use when irrigating a laceration, but plan on using at least ¹/₂ quart. In most cases, lacerations that you had to hold open in order to irrigate thoroughly should be held closed with wound closure strips or thin strips of tape after cleaning (see below). Apply a thin layer of antibiotic ointment, then a dressing and bandage.

Blisters result from sheer forces that cause aggressive rubbing of outer layers of skin against inner layers. The tough outer layer of skin separates from the sensitive inner layer. Fluid fills the space created between the layers. Blisters feel better when deflated, and controlled draining is far better than having them

SPLINTERS

Splinters should be removed as soon as possible. If the end is visible, grasp it with tweezers and pull the splinter out gently. If the end is buried, inspect closely and probe with your fingers until you find the orientation of the splinter, and push it toward the wound until the end is graspable. In the case of a deeply buried splinter, you may need to cut superficially with a sterilized blade to expose the splinter in order to remove it. In all cases, clean and dress any wounds.

rupture inside a dirty sock. To deflate, clean around the site thoroughly. Sterilize the point of a needle or knife, or use a sterile scalpel, and open the blister wide enough to easily massage the fluid out. Leaving the roof of the blister intact will make it feel better and heal faster. If the roof has been rubbed away, clean the wound. In all cases, apply a dressing that limits friction. Many commercial products are available that are ideal for this purpose. You can also build a moleskin doughnut, which is a rounded piece of moleskin with a hole cut in the center. Center the blister site in the hole and fill the hole with ointment. An antibiotic ointment is preferable, but any lubricating ointment will work. Tape or a strip of moleskin needs to be placed over the hole to keep the ointment in place.

Notes on Wound Cleaning

Proper wound cleaning, closing, and dressing will prevent most wound infections. Cleaning also speeds healing and reduces scarring. Start by washing your own hands and putting on protective gloves. The best method for cleaning is mechanical irrigation. Irrigation involves a high-pressure stream of an acceptable solution directed into the wound, best directed from an irrigation syringe. For most wounds, the best cleaning solution is disinfected water or at least potable water. Draw the water into the syringe, hold it about 2 inches above the wound and perpendicular to the wound, and push down forcefully on the plunger. Keep the wound tipped so the water runs out. Without an irrigation syringe, you can improvise by using a biking water bottle, melting a pinhole in the center of the lid of a standard water bottle, or punching a pinhole in a clean plastic bag. If you use something other than disinfected water, follow irrigation with a final flush of disinfected or potable water.

Large dirty wounds, wounds that expose bones, tendons, or ligaments, and wounds caused by animal bites should be left open. They are difficult to clean well enough to prevent infection. After irrigation, cover these wounds with sterile gauze. Exceptionally dirty wounds should be packed open with moist sterile gauze and covered with dry gauze to allow them to drain until a physician can be consulted.

Notes on Laceration Closure

If hair gets in the way of laceration closure, it can be carefully clipped short, but it should not be shaved. (Shaving may increase the risk of infection.) When using closure strips, apply one end of one strip to one side of the wound and another to the opposite side. By using the opposing strips as handles, you can pull the wound edges together, pulling the skin as close as possible to where it should lie naturally. Take your time, and avoid pulling the wound edges too tightly together or too loose, leaving a gap between the wound edges.

Notes on Wound Dressing

A *dressing* is the primary covering of a wound. It works best if it is sterile, non-adherent, porous, resistant to bacterial invasion, and easy to use. Wounds heal faster with less scarring if they are kept slightly moist with an antibiotic ointment or with a dressing that holds in the body's moisture, such as a micro-thin film dressing. Film dressings have the added advantages of being see-through and water-repellent. The dressing should completely cover the wound and ideally extend $1/2$ inch or so beyond the wound's edge. If you use a micro-thin film dressing, do *not* use an ointment.

Dressings, ideally, should be changed at least once every 24 hours, although transparent film dressings may be left in place until healing is complete.

The function of a *bandage* is to fix, protect, and further assist the dressing. It can be conforming gauze, tape, elastic wraps, clean cotton strips (such as you can cut from a shirt), or improvised out of anything available. The usefulness of a bandage is handicapped if it is too loose and dangerous if it is too tight. Do not hide rings or anything that could cut off circulation if swelling occurs. Check bandages often.

GUIDELINES FOR ASSESSMENT
AND TREATMENT OF BURNS

Burns may result from heat, chemical reactions, electricity (including lightning), and radiation (including solar radiation). Initial treatment needs to be given immediately following a quick initial assessment.

1. Remove the patient from the source of the burn.
2. Stop the burning process, the faster the better—within 30 seconds, if possible. Burns can continue to injure tissue for a surprisingly long time, even when the source of the burn has been removed. No first aid will be effective until the burning process has stopped. Smother flames, if appropriate, then cool the burn with water. Do not try to remove tar or melted plastic.
3. Be immediately suspicious of possible airway complications with burns to the face and/or neck, soot in the nose and/or mouth, singed facial hair, and a dry cough.

Specific burn treatment depends on your assessment of the depth and extent of the injury. Even though this assessment may be rough, it will be your basis for deciding how the patient will be managed, whether evacuation is required, and how urgently.

SUNBURN

The acute response to overexposure to ultraviolet light is burned skin. Prolonged exposure, over years, leads to premature skin aging and degenerative skin disorders such as cancer. First aid for sunburn includes cooling the skin, applying a moisturizer, taking ibuprofen for pain and inflammation, and staying out of direct sunlight. If blisters form, a doctor should be consulted. Prevention of sunburn includes wearing hats with brims and tightly woven clothing, sunblocks such as zinc oxide, and sunscreens with a high sun protection factor—SPF 15 or more. Be aware: You can burn on cloudy days, sunlight is most harmful between the hours of 10:00 a.m. and 3:00 p.m., and large amounts of UV light are reflected by snow and water.

Burn Depth

The deeper a burn penetrates into the skin, the more serious the injury.

Superficial burns: Skin is red, painful, and perhaps swollen.

Partial-thickness burns: Skin is red, painful, and swollen, and blisters form, sometimes more than an hour after cooling.

Full-thickness burns: Skin is painless and without blisters—although partial-thickness burns may surround full-thickness burns—and is pale (scalding) or charred (burns from fires).

Burn Extent

Use the "Rule of Palmar Surface": The patient's palmar surface—the inner surface of the palm and fingers—equals about 1 percent total body surface area (TBSA). The more TBSA burned, of course, the more serious the injury. *Note:* In addition to depth and extent, do not underestimate the value of pain as a burn assessment tool. If the patient is in a lot of pain, that is an indication of the need for a physician's care.

Burn Treatment

1. Gently wash the burn with slightly warm water and mild soap. Pat dry.
2. Leave the burn blisters intact.
3. Dress the burn with a thin layer of antibiotic ointment.
4. Cover the burn with a gauze pad or a thin layer of roll gauze, or apply clean clothing. Covering wounds reduces pain and evaporative losses.
5. Do not pack wounds or patient in ice.
6. Elevate burned extremities to minimize swelling. Swelling retards healing and encourages infection. Get the patient, as much as possible, to gently and regularly move burned areas.
7. If you have no ointment or dressings, leave the burn alone. The burn's surface will dry into a scab-like covering that provides a significant amount of protection.
8. Keep the patient warm.
9. Keep the patient well hydrated.

Note: When evacuation is imminent, do not redress or re-examine the burn. But if evacuation is distant, redress the injury twice a day by removing old dressings (you may have to soak off old dressings with clean, tepid water), rewashing (and removing the old ointment), and putting on a clean covering.

GUIDELINES FOR TREATMENT AND PREVENTION OF CHAFING

Chafing in the groin area and between the thighs can be treated with a layer of lubricating oil or ointment, such as petrolatum jelly (Vaseline) or cooking oil. It is messy but relieves the irritation.

Chafing is easier to prevent than treat. Consider the following:

1. Wear loose cotton pants and underwear to hike in when it is not too cold. Sweat gets absorbed, and dry skin chafes less often.
2. Apply a layer of lubricating ointment to chafe-prone areas prior to hiking.
3. Apply an antiperspirant to chafe-prone areas.

GUIDELINES FOR ASSESSMENT AND TREATMENT OF EAR, NOSE, AND TEETH PROBLEMS

Problems associated with an ear, the nose, or teeth are common and typically non-serious. It is important, however, to be able to recognize and appropriately treat a serious problem.

Ear

If something is lodged in the ear, do *not* use force to remove it. If it is small, it can often be rinsed out with water. An insect in the ear canal can be treated by instilling sweet oil, or any cooking oil, into the ear, which effectively decreases the insect's movement and may rinse the insect out or suffocate it until it can be removed by trained medical personnel.

Outer ear infections, or swimmer's ear, hurt more when you pull on the earlobe. Rinse the ear daily with a solution of 50 percent water and 50 percent vinegar or alcohol. If pain persists, seek trained medical help. Middle ear infections do not increase in pain when the earlobe is tugged and are often accompanied by vertigo. These infections require a physician's attention.

Nose

To stop a nosebleed, keep the patient sitting and leaning forward, and pinch the meaty part of the nose just below the nasal bone firmly shut. Hold it for 10 minutes. If the bleeding persists, pinch for another 10 minutes and repeat until the bleeding stops. Continued bleeding can be treated by packing the nostrils gently with gauze soaked with antibiotic ointment or a decongesting nasal spray. Most nosebleeds are not serious, but it is possible for noses to bleed from the back, and for blood to run down the throat. These posterior nosebleeds need a physician's attention and, therefore, rapid evacuation.

Trauma to the nose that causes deformity may be treated with cold packs. Nosebleeds that result from trauma can be very brisk, but generally stop within 15 to 20 minutes and usually do not reoccur; however, spontaneous nosebleeds may reoccur. Spontaneous bleeds will be prone to reoccur until a scab within the nose heals firmly, which takes about 10 days. Ask the patient *not* to blow their nose as this tends to remove the clot and restart the bleeding. It is best to seek professional help within 10 days if the nose is deformed by trauma.

Teeth

Where a filling has fallen out or a cavity has developed, pain usually first occurs when cold, food, or the tongue hits the spot. After rinsing the area clean, a drop of oil of cloves (eugenol) will ease the pain. A temporary filling is the best treatment until a dentist can be found. Temporary filling material is available for first aid kits. A temporary filling can be made from mixing zinc oxide powder and eugenol. To improvise, fill the cavity with candle wax, ski wax, or sugarless gum. Temporary filling material can also be used to hold a dislodged crown back in place.

GUIDELINES FOR PREVENTION

Consult your dentist at least one month prior to an extended backcountry trip or a journey to a foreign country to have potential problems identified and treated. Routine oral hygiene will prevent most trip-ruining dental problems: Floss once a day and brush twice a day with a soft-bristled toothbrush.

If a tooth is knocked out, there is a chance it can be salvaged if you can get it back in the empty socket. Hold the tooth by the crown and avoid touching the root. After rinsing the tooth with clean water (*do not* scrub it), press it gently back in. If it will not go back in, at least save it until you find a dentist. The best way

EYE PROBLEMS

If the patient complains of something in the eye, look closely and try to identify the object. If it is lodged, leave it alone and find a doctor. If it is large and lodged, protect the object to prevent it being bumped, and carry the patient out sitting at approximately a 45 degree angle. If it is small and loose, flush it out or dab it out with a soft cloth. Once loose objects are removed, the patient may complain that it still feels like something is there. The eye is probably scratched—typically not serious, but the eye will heal faster patched shut for 24 hours. A "black eye" is typically non-serious and self-limiting (and a cold pack on the eye will probably ease pain), but beware of injuries that produce visible cuts or any disturbance in vision— reasons to find a doctor. Swollen, red, itchy eyes with a colorful discharge are almost always infected. After flushing the eye with disinfected water, small amounts of antibiotic ointment may be placed in the eye several times a day. Ointments made for the eye are best. If the problem persists, it should be seen by a physician.

to store the tooth is for the person to hold the tooth in his or her mouth with obvious care being taken not to swallow it. If this is not practical, store the tooth in milk or 0.9 percent saline. If neither is possible, store the tooth in water.

An infected tooth is indicated by pain and swelling in the gum and cheek near the tooth. Discoloration of the gum may be visible. Cold packs on the cheek may give some relief. If evacuation is delayed, have the patient rinse her or his mouth several times a day with warm, salty water. Antibiotic therapy is usually required, and an evacuation without delay should be initiated.

GUIDELINES FOR TREATMENT AND PREVENTION OF SOME BITES

Common bites include those received from mosquitoes and ticks. Although primarily a nuisance, these bites may carry the risk of disease. Less common but potentially more dangerous are the bites of some snakes.

Mosquitoes

The itching from mosquito bites can be treated with topical agents available over the counter. In all cases, scratching should be avoided to prevent open wounds that may become a source of infection. Some mosquito bites carry the risk of West Nile virus. Flu-like illness (headache, muscle aches, low fever) that develops within 2 weeks of receiving mosquito bites should be evaluated by a physician.

Some mosquito bites can be prevented by avoiding exposure during prime biting times, usually dawn and dusk. Be sure tents have adequate netting on doors and windows. Set camps well away from high-risk areas: standing water, swampy ground, dense brush. Repellents that work with mosquitoes include products containing DEET, the most effective repellent. Concentrations of DEET higher than 30 percent do not improve repellency, but they do require reapplication less often. In the United States, products that contain picaridin are only available in 7 percent concentration. These repellents are effective for light infestations of flies, gnats, and mosquitoes. Some nonchemical repellents work for short periods of time. With all repellents, read and follow the directions on the labels. Treat clothing, tents, and sleeping bags with 0.5 percent permethrin every 6 weeks. Studies have shown that the combination of permethrin on clothing and an appropriate insect repellent on skin can prevent nearly 100 percent of bites from disease-bearing mosquitoes—and ticks.

Ticks

In the United States, ticks may carry one of at least eight diseases. Depending on the specific pathogen, the tick has to feed from several hours to several days to pass enough germs to cause disease. Any unexplained illness—or rash—that develops after removal of an embedded tick should be evaluated by a physician.

Ticks are repelled by many of the same repellents that keep mosquitoes from biting. Body checks for ticks should be performed twice daily when hiking and camping in tick-infested country. All ticks need to be removed immediately. Embedded ticks should be pulled out slowly with tweezers after grasping the tick perpendicular to the long axis of the tick and near the patient's skin line.

Snakes

Venomous snakes of the United States include the pit vipers and coral snakes. The risk of death from a bite is low. With all snake bites, keep the patient physically and emotionally calm, and gently wash the bite site. Splint bitten extremities and keep the bite site at approximately the level of the patient's heart. Do *not* cut, suck, apply a constricting band, or apply cold. Go for help. The patient should not walk unless it is unavoidable in evacuating the patient. The treatment of choice for snakebite is to get your car keys and drive the patient to a hospital. Snakebites need to be evaluated by a physician; they are puncture wounds that might cause infections, including tetanus.

GUIDELINES FOR ASSESSMENT AND TREATMENT OF WOUND INFECTION

Mild infection is indicated by pain, redness, swelling, and a little light-colored pus. These wounds should be recleaned, redressed, and monitored closely.

Monitor for signs of serious infection:

1. Increasing pain, redness, and swelling are primary indicators of serious infection.
2. Increasing heat at the site.

3. Pus increasing and growing darker in color.
4. Appearance of red streaks just under the skin near the wound.
5. Systemic fever.

Persons with signs of serious infection require rapid evacuation. If you see any signs of serious infection, allow the wound to reopen and let it drain. You may need to encourage the process with soaks in water as hot as the patient can tolerate. Pack the wound with moist, sterile gauze to keep it draining, and dress it with dry, sterile gauze. Wet-to-dry dressings encourage draining. Reclean and repack the wound twice a day during an extended evacuation.

GUIDELINES FOR PERSONAL AND CAMP HYGIENE

Maintaining a high level of personal and camp hygiene can reduce the risk of skin infections.
1. Use soap and water to wash hands at least once a day and before meal preparation. You can use a hand sanitizer after bowel movements and urinating.
2. Body washing is not mandatory but should be considered on extended trips and performed at least 200 feet from natural water sources. During cold or inclement weather, powdering the groin, underarms, and feet with talcum powder can provide protection from moisture and accumulating body odor and oils.

GUIDELINES FOR PREVENTION OF WOUNDS AND WOUND INFECTION

Standard safety precautions will prevent many wounds. Most wound infections can be prevented with adequate cleaning, dressing, and bandaging.

Blisters can be prevented by:

1. Wearing boots or shoes that fit and are broken in
2. Wearing a thin inner sock under a thicker outer sock
3. Treating "hot spots" *before* they become blisters
4. Taking off your boots to let your feet dry when you take a break from hiking

GUIDELINES FOR EVACUATION

Evacuate—you can go slow—any patient with a wound that cannot be closed in the field. Wounds that gape more than $1/2$ inch should not be closed in the field but instead evacuated for closure by a physician. Evacuate rapidly—go fast—any patient with a wound that:

1. Is heavily contaminated
2. Opens a joint space
3. Involves tendons or ligaments
4. Was caused by an animal bite
5. Is deep and on the face
6. Involves an impalement
7. Was caused by a crushing injury

Evacuate—you can go slow—any patient with an infected wound or skin infection that does not improve within 12 hours of treatment or that spreads to other parts of the body. Evacuate rapidly—go fast—any patient with signs and symptoms of a serious infection. If more than one person on the trip breaks out in skin boils or abscesses, be concerned about group contamination with MRSA, a serious staph infection, and immediately evacuate to seek professional medical care.

Evacuate all patients with serious burns to the face, neck, hands, feet, armpits, or groin, and all patients with full-thickness burns. Rapidly evacuate—go fast—any patient with burns threatening the airway, with partial- or full-thickness circumferential burns, and with blisters and/or full-thickness burns covering 10 percent TBSA.

8.

ABDOMINAL PROBLEMS

GENERAL INFORMATION

Abdominal pain and discomfort, a common wilderness problem, can have numerous sources, from mild and nonthreatening to serious and life-threatening. You may never know the source of the problem, but you must be able to manage mild problems and know when a problem is serious, requiring an evacuation.

General assessment includes asking the appropriate questions about the pain and/or discomfort. (Your questions need to provide you with the answers necessary to determine if the pain is serious.) Assessment may include pressing gently on the four quadrants of the abdomen with your hand flattened. Note this assessment on your report form and any changes over time.

GUIDELINES FOR ASSESSMENT
AND TREATMENT OF STOMACHACHE

Gastroenteritis, often called a stomachache, is an inflammation of the gastrointestinal tract. It can be caused by viruses, bacteria, or protozoa. Mild inflammations are characterized by gradually increasing widespread abdominal discomfort, often worse in the lower abdominal region. Intermittent cramping is common. Nausea and vomiting may occur. The patient should be kept well

FIELD WATER DISINFECTION

A lot of gastrointestinal distress can be avoided at home and abroad if you disinfect all drinking water. There are four methods that work:

1. Boiling will kill organisms that make people sick. In fact, the time it takes water to reach the boiling point, even at high altitudes, kills organisms. So, by the time water has reached the point of boiling, it is safe to drink.

2. Filters differ greatly in their ability to disinfect water. Some filter out only protozoa, such as *Giardia* and *Cryptosporidium*. Some filter out protozoa and bacteria. None filter out viruses, but some have an iodine-resin on the filter that may kill viruses. Choose carefully.

3. Chemicals can be added to water to kill harmful organisms. Products containing iodine or chlorine are generally the safest and most effective, but few chemicals

guarantee water safe from *Cryptosporidium* (with chlorine dioxide tablets being one exception). Iodine and chlorine are commercially available in several forms including tablets and solutions. If you have povidone-iodine solution in your first aid kit, it can be used to disinfect water. The solution is best measured with a dropper. Eight drops of povidone-iodine solution in a quart of warm, clear water and a 15-minute wait will give you a safe drink. For cold, clear water, double the drops and double the wait (16 drops for 30 minutes). For cloudy water, double the drops and triple the wait.

4. Devices that use ultraviolet light to disinfect water are highly effective if the water is not too cloudy or dirty. Cloudy and dirty water can be strained prior to using a UV light device to increase the effectiveness of the device.

hydrated, and a bland diet is recommended; avoid high-fat foods, spicy foods, dairy products, caffeine, and alcohol.

GUIDELINES FOR ASSESSMENT AND TREATMENT OF DIARRHEA

Diarrhea is frequent, loose, watery stools, often associated with gastroenteritis. Mild diarrhea can be treated with water, diluted clear fruit juices, or sports drinks. Persistent diarrhea requires more aggressive replacement of electrolytes lost in the stool. Oral rehydration solutions are best for treating serious diarrhea. You can make an oral rehydration solution by adding 1 teaspoon of salt and 8 teaspoons of sugar to a quart of water. The patient should drink about one-fourth of this solution every hour, along with all the water he or she will tolerate. Rice, grains, bananas, and potatoes are okay to eat. Fats, dairy products, caffeine, and alcohol should be avoided. Over-the-counter medications for watery diarrhea are available.

GUIDELINES FOR ASSESSING SERIOUS ABDOMINAL PAIN

1. Pain persists for more than 12 hours, especially if the pain is constant.
2. Pain localizes, and especially if the pain involves guarding (the patient voluntarily or involuntarily protects the area), tenderness, abdominal rigidity, and/or distention.

3. Pain increases with movement, jarring, or foot strike when walking.
4. Blood appears in the vomit, feces, or urine. In vomit, blood may look like coffee grounds; in stool, it may look a tar-like black, and in urine blood appears a reddish color.
5. Nausea, vomiting, and/or diarrhea persist for longer than 24 hours, especially if the patient is unable to stay well hydrated.
6. A fever rises above 102 degrees Fahrenheit, which may present clinically as chilling or shivers.
7. Pain is associated with the signs and symptoms of pregnancy or vaginal bleeding.
8. Pain is associated with the signs and symptoms of shock.

GUIDELINES FOR PERSONAL AND CAMP HYGIENE

Poor hygiene in the wilderness may be the primary source of abdominal problems.

1. Use soap and water or hand sanitizer to wash/clean hands prior to food preparation.
2. Do not share personal items such as spoons, cups, water bottles, and lip balm.
3. Do not use a personal spoon to take food from a pot, and do *not* reach into a communal food bag, such as a bag of trail mix, with your hand.
4. Keep kitchen gear clean.

ABDOMINAL INJURIES

Abdominal injuries may be generally classified in two categories:

1. Blunt trauma, a closed abdominal injury caused by a forceful blow to the abdomen.
2. Penetrating trauma, an open abdominal injury caused by an object being forced into the abdomen. The extent of injury is often difficult to assess in the wilderness—or anywhere, for that matter. No other region of the human body has more potential to conceal serious blood loss.

Generally, treat for shock. Stay alert to the possibility of vomiting. Patients suffering blunt trauma should be kept in the position of comfort they choose—if no other injuries prevent this—and kept warm. If you are involved in the evacuation, comfort and warmth should be extended to patients during the carry-out. In general, nothing should be given to them by mouth, but on an extended evacuation, sips of water, preferably cool, may be necessary to prevent dehydration.

The immediate seriousness of any penetrating abdominal injury, as with blunt trauma, is determined by what got damaged inside and how bad it is bleeding. With severe bleeding, shock is imminent and immediate evacuation the only chance of salvation. Over time the risk of infection may be high. General treatment of the patient is the same as for a patient suffering blunt abdominal trauma. Specific treatment will vary somewhat depending on the soft tissue involvement. External bleeding should be controlled. Wounds should be cleaned and bandaged. Impaled objects, in almost all cases, should be stabilized in place.

An evisceration, in short-term care, should be covered with sterile dressings soaked in disinfected water to prevent drying out. Check the dressings every 2 hours to make sure they stay moist. Cover the moist dressings with thick, dry dressings, and rapidly evacuate the patient. In long-term care (more than several hours), the exposed intestines will do better if they are flushed clean with disinfected water and "teased" back inside by gently pulling the wound open. If teasing does not work, you may have to gently push the exposed loops of intestine back inside the abdominal cavity. Then clean and bandage the wound.

5. Do not eat leftover food unless it can be stored cool and completely reheated.
6. Disinfect all drinking water via boiling (water is safe at the point it reaches a rolling boil), chemical disinfectants such as chlorine dioxide, filtration (or a combination of filtering and iodine or chlorine), or an ultraviolet light device.

GUIDELINES FOR EVACUATION

Evacuate—you can go slow—any patient with persistent abdominal discomfort. Evacuate rapidly—go fast—any patient with signs and symptoms of a serious abdominal problem.

9.
HYPOTHERMIA

GENERAL INFORMATION

The human body constantly generates heat via metabolism. At rest, heat is generated via basal metabolic activity. Exercise increases metabolic heat production dramatically, the rate depending on the fitness of the person and the level of activity. Some heat may be absorbed from external heat sources (such as the sun or a campfire). Heat is constantly shed via radiation from skin, conduction via contact with cold material such as the ground, convection via the movement of air across skin, and evaporation of moisture from skin. The human thermoregulatory system typically balances heat gain and heat loss to keep the body core temperature around 99.6 degrees F (98.6 degrees oral temperature).

Hypothermia is a lowering of the body's core temperature to a point where normal brain and/or muscle function is impaired. This condition may be mild, moderate, or life-threateningly severe.

GUIDELINES FOR ASSESSMENT AND TREATMENT

Mild hypothermia manifests itself in a patient through shivers, inability to perform complex tasks (fumbles), confusion, apathy, sluggish thinking (grumbles), slurred speech (mumbles), and altered gait (stumbles)—sometimes referred to as "the umbles."

Moderate hypothermia manifests itself in a patient through worsening of the umbles and uncontrollable violent shivering.

In a patient with severe hypothermia, shivering stops. The patient may experience increasing muscle rigidity, stupor progressing to coma, decreasing pulse and respirations to the point where they are undetectable (but still present!).

Management can be divided, for simplicity, into two categories: treatment for mild and moderate hypothermia, and treatment for severe hypothermia.

The mild-moderate hypothermia patient is still trying to warm up internally. The patient can talk, eat, and shiver. Change the environment so the heat being produced internally is not lost. Get the patient out of wet clothes and into something dry, and out of wind and cold and into some kind of shelter, even if the only shelter available is the protection of waterproof, windproof clothing. Cover the patient's head and neck. If the patient can eat and drink, give her or him simple carbohydrates (such as candy or sugary drinks) to stoke the inner fire. Fluids are more important than solids to a cold person. A warm, sweet drink will add a negligible amount of heat but a lot of simple sugar for energy plus fluid. Even cold fluids are better than no fluids. If the patient can still exercise easily, you may keep moving after initial treatment. If the patient cannot exercise easily, do all you can to encourage entrapment of inner heat production: insulate the patient from the ground, bundle in dry insulation, snuggle with warm people, place hot water bottles near the heart and in the armpits (but not against naked skin), use chemical heat packs as

PARTIAL-THICKNESS FROSTBITE

When this occurs, skin is pale and numb, but it moves when you press on it. Begin passive warming immediately. In the field cover the cold body part with warm body parts. Cover your nose with your warm hand, stick your cold hand against your warm stomach, put your cold toes against the warm stomach of a friend. Do not rub the cold skin. Do not place cold skin near a hot heat source because numb tissue is very susceptible to heat injury. Give aspirin or ibuprofen, if available, and lots of water to drink.

Skin that looks okay after warming is usually okay. If blisters form after warming, a physician should be consulted as soon as possible. In the meantime, two things should be remembered:

1. Leave the bubble intact. It protects the underlying tissue and creates less of a chance for infection.
2. Blisters freeze quickly, multiplying the damage. Be careful to prevent freezing by protecting the injured tissue from exposure to cold.

FULL-THICKNESS FROSTBITE

Skin is pale and numb—and hard. A patient can still travel on frozen feet, making an evacuation speedier. Although the frozen parts benefit from thawing as soon as possible, normal field conditions often make warming of deep frostbite impractical, and the patient overall is likely to do better with a faster evacuation.

If refreezing is unlikely, and you have the means available, you can best treat full-thickness frostbite by rapid warming in water of approximately 99 to 102 degrees F. Too hot and heat damage occurs. Too cold and thawing is too slow for maximum benefit. Warming is usually accomplished in 30 to 40 minutes, but it is better to err on the side of caution and warm longer than necessary rather than less than necessary. Place soft cotton between thawed digits, but otherwise contact with anything should be avoided. Pain is often intense, and painkillers may be started prior to thawing. Aspirin or ibuprofen, following the regimen suggested on the bottle, started as soon as possible seems to reduce the extent of damage to tissue. Keep the patient well hydrated. Prevention of refreezing is of paramount importance. Find a doctor as soon as possible.

Hypothermia Wrap

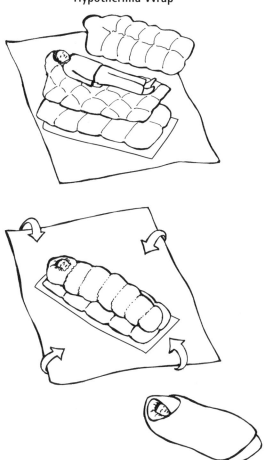

you would hot water bottles, and wait until the patient returns to normal.

The severe hypothermia patient is semi-conscious or unconscious and has stopped shivering. She or he has lost the ability to generate an appreciable amount of heat. Handle the patient gently—roughness can overload a cold heart and stop it. If breathing is undetectable, perform rescue breathing for at least 3 minutes prior to any movement. Remove clothing and bundle the patient up in as much dry insulation as possible. Insulate well from the ground. Wrap hot water bottles or heat packs in a dry sock or shirt and place them appropriately as with mild hypothermia. Finish with a vapor barrier—a tent fly, sheet of plastic, or garbage bags—something to trap any heat still left in the patient. The final product is a cocoon, a "hypothermia wrap" open only to the mouth and nose. Do not try to force food or drink. Treat for severe hypothermia even if the patient appears dead. *No patient is dead, as far as you are concerned, unless he or she is warm and dead.* Call for help immediately—do *not* try to evacuate the patient by any means other than gentle.

GUIDELINES FOR PREVENTION

It is far easier to maintain core temperature than to regain core temperature, so:
1. Wear clothing that retains body heat even when wet. Do not wear cotton clothing if the temperature could drop below 77 degrees F.

2. Stay dry by wearing layers of clothing, taking off layers before sweating starts, and adding them back before chilling occurs.
3. Stay well hydrated.
4. Eat regularly, especially carbohydrates.
5. Maintain a pace that prevents overexertion. Rest often.
6. In a group, watch each other for signs of hypothermia. Treat early, and if one person is treated, treat everyone.

GUIDELINES FOR EVACUATION

Patients who recover from mild to moderate hypothermia may remain in the field. Evacuate rapidly—go fast (but with extreme gentleness)—any patient with severe hypothermia.

10.

HEAT PROBLEMS

GENERAL INFORMATION

"Heat illness" describes a range of problems associated with a rise in air temperature—everything from the fatigue of heat exhaustion to the life threat of heat stroke. In addition to rising temperatures, other factors increase your risk of heat illness including:

1. high humidity
2. being overweight
3. being very young or very old
4. being unaccustomed to heat
5. taking certain drugs, such as antihistamines (consult your physician)
6. being dehydrated—often the most important factor

GUIDELINES FOR ASSESSMENT AND TREATMENT OF HEAT EXHAUSTION

Heat exhaustion is a result of heat stress, water and electrolyte loss (most often via sweat), and less than adequate hydration. The patient has usually been exercising and sweating out water and salt, and now feels very tired. Skin may appear pale and sweaty or flushed, and the patient complains of a headache, perhaps nausea and sometimes vomiting. Thirst is usual, as well as a decreased

HEAT CRAMPS

Sometimes associated with heat exhaustion are heat cramps, most commonly occurring in the large muscles of the legs and sometimes extending up into the abdomen. Though the discomfort may be great, the problem is rarely serious. Treatment includes rest and drinking water with a pinch of salt added per quart or with a salty snack. Oral rehydration salts or a sports drink will work. Once feeling well, the patient may continue. But if the cramps return, the sufferer should take the rest of the day off. Overworking depleted muscles can lead to a serious injury.

urine output. Dizziness may strike when the patient stands quickly. An elevated heart rate and respiratory rate are common. The core temperature with heat exhaustion may have risen a few degrees but more often not at all.

Treatment is suggested by the name of the condition: Exhaustion calls for rest, preferably in a cool, shady spot. Replace lost fluids with water and lost salt by adding a pinch to a quart of water or by eating salty snacks. Oral rehydration salts or a sports drink will work. Do not use salt tablets—they are too concentrated. To increase the rate of cooling, the patient may be wet down and fanned. A drowsy patient may be allowed to sleep. When the patient feels okay, he or she may continue.

GUIDELINES FOR ASSESSMENT
AND TREATMENT OF HEAT STROKE

Heat stroke occurs when a patient is producing core heat faster than it can be shed. The patient may be overexerting and/or seriously dehydrated, and the core temperature rises to 105 degrees F or more. Disorientation and bizarre personality changes are common signs. Skin turns hot and red, and sometimes (but far from always) dry. Look for a fast heart rate, fast breathing, and complaints of a headache.

Heat stroke is a temperature problem. The patient is too hot inside. Once a human brain gets too hot, it is a true emergency! Only rapid cooling will save the patient. The ideal treatment is to take off any heat-retaining clothing and immerse the patient in cold water until he or she regains consciousness. Immersion is recommended when a large enough source of water is available. Without a large source of cold water, take off any heat-retaining clothes and drench the patient with cold water. Concentrate cooling efforts on the head and neck. Cold packs may be used on the neck, armpits, and groin, and on the hands and feet. Fan the patient constantly to increase evaporation. Monitor the patient closely and cease cooling efforts when a normal mental status returns. When, or if, the patient is able to accept and drink cold water, give it. Do not give fever-reducing drugs. The patient must see a physician as soon as possible, even if she or he appears to have recovered. During evacuation, a careful watch on the patient should be maintained. Relapses are common.

GUIDELINES FOR ASSESSMENT AND TREATMENT OF HYPONATREMIA

Hyponatremia results when the blood sodium level falls too low to maintain normal body function. This is usually the result of drinking more than enough water while failing to eat.

Common complaints include headache, weakness, fatigue, lightheadedness, muscle cramps, nausea with or without vomiting, sweaty skin, normal core temperature, normal or slightly elevated pulse and respirations, and a rising level of anxiety. The patient appears to have heat exhaustion. But if you treat it like heat exhaustion—just add water—you are harming the hyponatremia patient. More severe symptoms of hyponatremia include disorientation, irritability, and combativeness—which gives the problem a more common name: water intoxication. Untreated, the ultimate result will be seizures, coma, and death.

Heat exhausted patients typically have a low output of yellowish urine (urinating every 6 to 8 hours) combined with thirst. Hyponatremia patients have urinated recently and the urine was probably clear. Hyponatremia patients will also claim to have been drinking a lot of water, and they deny thirst.

Patients with mild to moderate symptoms and a normal mental status may be treated in the field: Rest in shade with no fluid intake and a gradual intake of salty foods while the kidneys reestablish a sodium balance. Once a patient develops hunger and thirst combined with normal urine output, the problem is solved. Restriction of fluids for someone who is well hydrated, fortunately, is harmless. Patients with an altered mental status require rapid evacuation to a medical facility; there is no question.

GUIDELINES FOR PREVENTION

1. Stay well hydrated. A hydration routine should be based on discipline and *not* on thirst. Consume 400 to 600 milliliters of water (roughly ½ quart) about 2 hours prior to periods of exercise. During exercise consume 150 to 350 milliliters of water (roughly ¼ to ⅓ of a quart) for every 15 to 20 minutes of exercise. If exercise lasts for more than 1 hour, the addition of a solution of 4 to 8 percent carbohydrates and electrolytes (such as a sports drink) is recommended. Fluid replacement after exercise is also vitally important. Urine output should be clear and relatively copious, an indication of adequate hydration. It is practically impossible to drink too much water as long as you eat regularly, preferably low-salt snacks. Avoid alcohol and caffeinated drinks.

2. Wear baggy, loosely woven clothing that allows evaporation of sweat. Keep your head covered and your face shaded.

3. Keep yourself fit, and allow time for acclimatization when you are new to a hot environment. Go slow the first few days and avoid exercising during the hottest times of day.

4. Beware of drugs that increase your risk of heat illness, including alcohol and antihistamines.

5. Rest often in the shade.

GUIDELINES FOR EVACUATION

Evacuate—go slow—any patient that does not fully recover from heat exhaustion or mild hyponatremia. Evacuate rapidly—go fast—any patient who has an altered mental status due to heat exhaustion or hyponatremia.

11.
LIGHTNING

GENERAL INFORMATION

Lightning strikes can cause harm via a direct strike (the patient is hit), splash (the strike jumps from its direct target to hit a patient), ground current (the electrical charge radiates out from its strike point through the ground, reaching the patient), long conductors (the patient is touching a long conductor such as a fence when the conductor is hit), or blast injury (the patient is thrown by the exploding air).

Lightning strikes may produce several types of injuries including:

1. Cardiac and/or pulmonary arrest
2. Neurological problems such as loss of responsiveness, paralysis, or seizures
3. Blindness, often temporary
4. Deafness, often temporary
5. Burns, typically superficial and feathery or fern-like
6. Trauma from being thrown

GUIDELINES FOR ASSESSMENT AND TREATMENT

When the scene is safe (lightning will strike twice in the same place), patients require a full assessment. Rescue breathing or

CPR should be started immediately if needed. Other injuries require appropriate treatment.

GUIDELINES FOR PREVENTION

1. *Know local weather patterns.* Lightning storms, in general, tend to roll in quickly in the afternoon of summer months.
2. *Plan turn-around times* in lightning-prone areas, and stick to the plan.
3. *Plot storms.* When the flash of lightning precedes the boom of thunder by 5 seconds, the storm is approximately 1 mile away. Follow the 30-30 rule: Seek a safe location when the storm is no less than 6 miles (30 seconds from flash to boom) away, and stay in the safe location for 30 minutes after the storm passes.
4. *Find a safe spot.* Move downhill. Avoid high places, high objects (such as tall trees), open places, damp caves, over-hangs, flood zones, places obviously struck in the past, and long conductors (such as fences). Metal conducts electricity, so avoid metal. Remove any metallic frame packs and do not stay near them. Water also conducts electricity, so if you are boating or swimming, get to land and move away from the shore. Seek uniform cover, such as low rolling hills or trees of about the same size, a low spot among rocks, or deep dry caves. You can take shelter in a steel-framed building or a hard-topped motor vehicle. In a building, avoid telephones, avoid contact with anything connected to electrical power,

and avoid contact with metal. In a vehicle, keep the windows rolled up and avoid contact with metal parts.

5. *Assume a safe position when outdoors.* Squat or sit in a tight body position on insulating material. Do not lie down. If you feel your hair stand on end or your skin get tingly, cover your ears with your hands, close your eyes, and get your head close to your knees. Spread groups out, 100 feet or more between individuals, but try to keep everyone in sight.

6. *Pick safe campsites*, campsites that meet the criteria of a "safe spot" as mentioned above.

7. *Be sure everyone in a group understands these guidelines.*

Lightning Safety Position

GUIDELINES FOR EVACUATION

Evacuate rapidly—go fast—any patient who has been struck by lightning, even if he or she appears to have recovered soon after the injury. Serious problems sometimes develop later.

LIGHTNING DE-MYTHED

- Lightning *will* strike in the same place twice and many more times than twice.
- Lightning is *not* stored by a human body.
- Lightning may strike *before,* during, and *after* a storm.
- Lightning *can* cause serious internal injury while leaving no external signs.
- Lightning is not attracted to metal, but metal does conduct the charge extremely well.
- Lightning does strike vehicles. Rubber tires on a car or truck do nothing to protect you. But electricity stays on the outside of metal, taking the path of least resistance, making the inside of a car or truck safe if the windows are rolled up.

12.
ALTITUDE ILLNESSES

GENERAL INFORMATION

Altitude illnesses are the result of insufficient oxygen in the blood (hypoxia) due to decreasing barometric pressure as elevation is gained. As altitude is gained, air grows "thinner" and less oxygen is inhaled with each breath.

GUIDELINES FOR ASSESSMENT AND TREATMENT

Altitude illnesses range from a mild discomfort to an immediate threat to life.

Acute Mountain Sickness (AMS)

Signs and symptoms of acute mountain sickness (AMS) in someone who has recently arrived at an altitude of 8,000 feet or more include headache, loss of normal appetite, nausea (with or without vomiting), insomnia, and lassitude (unusual weakness, weariness, or exhaustion). The syndrome resembles an alcohol hangover. There are no characteristic physical findings. Signs and symptoms of AMS may appear below 8,000 feet but are then more often the result of a problem other than AMS such as dehydration or heat illness.

Basic treatment is to descend or to stop ascent and wait for improvement before going higher. Continuing ascent in the presence of symptoms is not recommended. After stopping the ascent, more advanced treatment consists of administering supplemental oxygen, which is especially helpful during sleep. Aspirin or acetaminophen is useful for headaches. Treatment of the illness, rather than just the symptoms, requires acetazolamide. The treatment dose is 250 milligrams twice a day. Acetazolamide speeds acclimatization and cures the illness for many people. An alternative to acetazolamide for persons who are sulfa allergic is dexamethasone (4 milligrams/6 to 8 hours). A response, in all cases, is usually seen within 12 to 24 hours. If the illness progresses, descent is mandatory. Persons going to an altitude greater than 8,000 feet should discuss obtaining personal prescriptions of acetazolamide and/or dexamethasone with their personal physician.

High Altitude Cerebral Edema (HACE)

Untreated, mild illness may progress to a more severe condition. The most important early sign of this progression is often ataxia (a loss of coordination). An ataxic patient cannot walk a straight line or stand straight with feet together and eyes closed. Ataxia typically indicates the patient is progressing into a severe form of altitude illness known as high altitude cerebral edema (HACE). HACE is caused by fluid collecting within the brain, increasing pressure on the brain until it fails to function properly and eventually fails to function, resulting in death.

Signs and symptoms include a severe headache unrelieved by rest and medication, bizarre changes in personality, perhaps seizures and/or coma. *Severely ill patients need to descend as soon as possible.* In addition to descent, the best treatment is supplemental oxygen. Treatment may also include the drug dexamethasone (8 to 10 milligrams initially, followed by 4 milligrams every 6 hours until symptoms subside). Other possible treatments include the use of a Gamow bag (a portable hyperbaric chamber). Do not use a Gamow bag instead of descent.

HIGH ALTITUDE PULMONARY EDEMA (HAPE)

Severe altitude illness may present as high altitude pulmonary edema (HAPE), fluid collecting in the air spaces of the lungs. If enough fluid collects, the patient cannot breathe adequately, and death may result.

The signs and symptoms of HAPE often appear initially as a dry cough, soon followed by complaints of shortness of breath even at rest. Shortness of breath becomes more pronounced, with perhaps complaints of chest pain. The cough becomes productive, producing frothy sputum early and reddish sputum later. *Severely ill patients need to descend as soon as possible.* A descent of 1,000 to 1,500 feet may produce remarkable results. In addition to descent, the best treatment is supplemental oxygen. Use the Gamow bag, if it is available, but not instead of descent.

GUIDELINES FOR PREVENTION

Most altitude illnesses are preventable. The following guidelines reduce the incidence and severity of illness. Although these measures do not guarantee anyone freedom from illness, they are highly recommended, especially for those without altitude experience.

1. Staged ascent: The most critical factor in preventing illness is to gain altitude no faster than your body can acclimatize (physiologically adjust) to the decrease in barometric pressure. Acclimatize by gradually increasing the altitude of overnight camps. If possible, the first camp should be no higher than 8,000 feet, with an increase of no more than 1,000 to 1,500 feet per night. If a trip is started at higher than 9,000 feet, two nights should be spent acclimatizing at that altitude before proceeding higher. Proceed higher during the day, if you wish, but return to a lower elevation to sleep (climb high, sleep low).

2. High-carbohydrate diet: A diet of at least 70 percent carbohydrates reduces symptoms of AMS by about 30 percent at altitudes higher than approximately 16,000 feet, and can be started 1 to 2 days prior to reaching 16,000 feet.

3. Appropriate exercise level: Until acclimatized, exercise moderately, avoiding excessive shortness of breath and fatigue.

4. Hydration: To offset increased fluid losses at high altitudes, stay well hydrated.

5. Drugs to prevent illness: Several drugs can lessen the symptoms of illness. However, their use is not recommended as a routine measure. Persons going to altitudes greater than 8,000 feet should discuss the use of medications to prevent altitude illness with their physician. Acetazolamide reduces the symptoms of AMS by about 75 percent and is considered the drug of choice for prevention of AMS. The dose of acetazolamide for adults is 125 milligrams twice a day, starting the day of ascent. The dose for children is 5 milligrams per kilogram of child's weight per day, up to the adult dose of 125 milligrams twice daily. Since acetazolamide is a diuretic, the increase in urine fluid loss needs to be replaced. Dexamethasone can be used to prevent AMS either for those who cannot take acetazolamide or for a rapid ascent to very high altitude, such as flying to higher than 14,000 feet. The dosage for adults is 4 milligrams orally every 6 to 8 hours. Starting the medication 2 to 4 hours prior to ascent is probably adequate, although the exact timing for beginning and discontinuing the medication has not yet been established. Nifedipine may prevent HAPE in HAPE-susceptible individuals. The prophylactic dose of nifedipine is 30 or 60 milligrams (extended release formation) per day to be taken during the ascent phase of the expedition and for 3 additional days at altitude.

Note: The use of sleeping aids is strongly discouraged above 10,000 feet because they cause a decrease in respiratory drive, which may predispose an individual to AMS.

Note: No drug should be taken, even if available, without directions from a physician. Persons going to an altitude higher than 8,000 feet should discuss obtaining personal prescriptions of acetazolamide, nifedipine, and/or dexamethasone with their personal physician.

GUIDELINES FOR EVACUATION

Patients with AMS should not continue to ascend until the symptoms resolve, but they do not require evacuation unless the symptoms do not resolve. Evacuation requires a loss of altitude. Patients with HACE or HAPE require a rapid—go fast—evacuation to a lower altitude (at least 1,000 to 1,500 feet) and evaluation as soon as possible by a physician.

13.

SUBMERSION INCIDENTS

GENERAL INFORMATION

Drowning accounts for several thousand deaths annually in the United States. Often those incidents would have been easily preventable had the persons involved understood and mitigated the risks. Drowning risks arise from activities as diverse as fording streams, seining for bait, swimming, snorkeling, scuba diving, surfing, and boating. Sometimes the victim is a poor swimmer who panics after becoming exhausted by swimming too far or fighting against a current. Such victims may call out for help and reach for a rescue aid. However, other active drowning victims, such as a non-swimmer stepping off a ledge into water or falling from a floating air mattress, will not be able to call for help or move even a few feet to safety. They typically submerge in less than a minute. Still other victims may submerge without warning due to seizures, strokes, or sudden cardiac arrest. Unconscious victims typically sink part way or all the way to the bottom rather than floating at the surface. Timely recognition of a person in trouble is vital to successful rescue and treatment. Such recognition requires careful, deliberate, uninterrupted scanning of everyone in an in-water activity.

A person struggling to remain at the surface will often ingest water. The swallowed water may later lead to vomiting during resuscitation attempts. Once victims are unable to keep their airway above the surface of the water, their breathing reflex results in water aspiration. Most people have an involuntary constriction of the muscles of the upper airway, a laryngospasm, which initially keeps large amounts of water out of the lungs. Asphyxia, an inadequate intake of oxygen, causes a loss of consciousness. Respiratory arrest and then cardiac arrest follow. Brain damage and death usually occur within a few minutes. However, in some cold water drownings, successful resuscitation has been performed after much longer periods.

At some point the laryngospasm relaxes, and water enters the lungs. Details differ between fresh water and salt water incidents, but transfer of oxygen from the lungs may be dangerously compromised. Aspiration of even a small amount of water requires prompt medical follow-up even if a submerged victim responds promptly to resuscitation.

GUIDELINES FOR RECOVERING A DROWNING VICTIM

Victim assists during a planned swimming activity in safe water conditions should be relatively safe and easy. Rescue aids should be gathered and procedures discussed prior to the activity. The following guidelines are recommended for getting a drowning person safely out of the water. Don't neglect to monitor the safety of everyone else in the water when attention is focused on an individual in trouble.

1. *Reach* with your hand, foot, paddle, or other extension device that allows you to remain safely on land.
2. For active victims, *throw* a flotation device or line within the grasp of the victim.
3. *Row* to the victim, or access the person in some sort of water-craft, using reaching or throwing devices as appropriate.
4. *Go.* Good swimmers with water rescue training may swim a flotation aid to an active victim. Recovery of an unconscious victim may require a surface dive and contact tow. In turbid water, limit the water depth and/or require participants to wear flotation devices to make recovery easier.

The same *reach, throw, row, go* progression is used in unsafe water conditions, but the risk to the rescuer may become unacceptable. Swift-water rescue of a kayaker pinned in heavy white-water calls for expertise from specialized training. Wilderness groups should only undertake activities for which they have proper training.

GUIDELINES FOR TREATMENT

Once the patient is safely accessible, check for an airway and breathing. If necessary, begin rescue breathing. Rescue breathing should be initiated as soon as possible, even with rescuers standing in shallow water, if appropriate. There is no value in attempting to clear the patient's lungs of water, but be ready to roll him or her to clear the airway if water or vomit comes up. Check for signs of a beating heart, and begin CPR if necessary. If the patient is breathing, or resumes breathing, treat for shock, hypothermia, or other conditions as appropriate. A potentially severe condition may have been the cause of the person's distress in the water.

Diving headfirst into shallow water is a major cause of sports-related spinal injury. If a person exhibits signs of a spinal injury in the water, then minimize movement if the person is breathing. If breathing is absent, rescue breathing and CPR as needed take precedence. Techniques for providing in-line stabilization in the water for both face-up and face-down victims are covered in water rescue courses.

Scuba diving introduces risks from breathing compressed air. Certified scuba divers are trained to avoid, recognize, and arrange treatment for such problems. Treatment may require transport to a hyperbaric chamber.

GUIDELINES FOR PREVENTION

1. All swimming and boating activities should be supervised by a mature, conscientious adult trained to respond to water-related emergencies.
2. Everyone should be screened prior to the activity for chronic or temporary medical conditions that may require special precautions in or on the water.
3. Anyone involved in water-related activities should be able to easily swim at least 100 yards and to demonstrate an effective resting stroke. Those unable to do so should be

restricted to shallow water for swimming activities. Boating activities for poor swimmers should be limited to stable craft on calm water where there is little likelihood of capsize. They should be accompanied by a buddy who is a good swimmer experienced in that craft.

4. All swimming activity should take place in an area that has been investigated and determined safe for swimming.
5. Swimmers should always be under observation by both a buddy and a prepared rescue team.
6. Headfirst diving into shallow water should be prohibited.
7. Everyone involved in boating activities should wear a Coast Guard approved life jacket that fits and is adjusted properly.
8. Everyone involved in whitewater activities should have proper training and wear an approved helmet.
9. No one should swim or participate in water-based activities under the influence of any mind-altering substance.

GUIDELINES FOR EVACUATION

Evacuate rapidly—go fast—any patient who was unconscious, no matter how short a time, during a submersion incident, any patient who may have aspirated water, and any patient with signs and symptoms of respiratory problems after a submersion incident due to the possibility of the problems becoming a threat to life.

14.
ALLERGIES AND ANAPHYLAXIS

GENERAL INFORMATION

The human body's immune system produces and releases histamines and other substances in response to the presence of foreign allergens. An allergic reaction is an overproduction and excessive release of these same substances. Allergens can be ingested, inhaled, injected, or absorbed, and they include foods and drugs, pollen, bee venom, and plant oils.

GUIDELINES FOR ASSESSMENT AND TREATMENT

For simplicity, allergic reactions can be divided into two stages: non-life-threatening and life-threatening. Non-life-threatening reactions are characterized by stuffy noses, flushed and itchy skin, hay fever signs and symptoms (such as runny nose, itchy eyes, sneezing, and coughing), swelling (at a bite site), and/or hives (reddish bumps or wheals that appear suddenly on skin). They can be treated in the field with an antihistamine.

A severe reaction, known as anaphylaxis, is a true emergency! There may be the signs and symptoms of a non-life-threatening reaction. Anaphylaxis may then produce shock but is more often typified by extreme difficulty breathing, causing the sufferer to be unable to speak or to speak only in one- or two-word clusters.

Swelling of the face, lips, tongue, and perhaps the hands and feet are indicative. These signs and symptoms can appear in as little as 5 minutes and most often within 45 minutes to 1 hour. Death is imminent. Anaphylaxis is reversible only by an immediate injection of epinephrine (adrenaline). Epinephrine reverses the effects of an overproduction of histamines. Injectable epinephrine is available commercially, and by prescription only, in spring-loaded syringes that function when pressed into the thigh. You may need to assist someone with the injection. Injections can be repeated if either the first one fails or a relapse occurs.

Use of EpiPen

The EpiPen is an auto-injection system with one injection available per box. It is available in adult and child doses. Using the EpiPen involves three simple steps:

1. Pull off the safety cap.
2. Place the black tip on the outer thigh, preferably against the skin, but it can be used through thin clothing.
3. Make sure your thumb is *not* over the end of the device, and push the unit against the thigh until it clicks, and hold it in place for a count of ten.

EpiPen

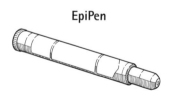
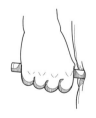

Use of Twinject

The Twinject has two injections of epinephrine available in one device, the first dose delivered automatically, and the second delivered manually. It is available in adult and child doses. Using the Twinject involves these steps:

1. Remove the device from the hard case.
2. Remove the green cap, labeled 1. You will see a red tip.
3. Remove the green cap, labeled 2.
4. Make sure your thumb is *not* over the end of the device, then place the red tip against the outer thigh, press down hard until the needle enters the thigh (it will go through clothing), and hold for a count of ten.
5. If you need a second injection, unscrew and remove the red tip, carefully avoiding the needle.
6. Grab the blue plastic and remove the syringe from the barrel.
7. Remove the yellow collar from the syringe.
8. Push the needle into the thigh and depress the plunger all the way to inject the second dose.
9. Store the used syringe in the hard case.

Twinject

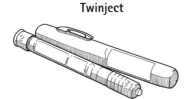

After injection of epinephrine, and when the patient can breathe and swallow easily, an oral antihistamine should be given following the directions on the label, to maintain the suppression of the overproduction of histamines. The patient should also be kept well hydrated.

Note: The use of any drug in the field should be after consultation with a physician and under his or her specific directions. Consult your physician prior to a wilderness trip.

Everyone who knows they are susceptible to severe allergic reactions should carry injectable epinephrine. Epinephrine can be ruined by extremes of cold and heat and needs to be protected from these extremes.

GUIDELINES FOR PREVENTION

Every precaution should be taken to avoid contact with allergens. Trip leaders who know party members suffer the possibility of a severe reaction should attempt to avoid taking known allergens on a trip. Individuals on trips who are susceptible to anaphylaxis should carry at least three injections of epinephrine.

GUIDELINES FOR EVACUATION

Mild to moderate reactions that can be managed in the field do not require evacuation. Anyone treated for anaphylaxis should be evacuated rapidly—go fast. During evacuation, the patient should be well hydrated and kept on a regimen of oral antihistamines.

15.
WILDERNESS FIRST AID KITS

GENERAL INFORMATION

The perfect wilderness first aid kit does not exist. Despite your best efforts at planning, some day you will want something that is not there and/or discover you've carried an item for years and never used it. When considering the contents of a kit, take into account:

1. The environment (such as altitude)
2. The number of people who will depend on the kit
3. The number of days the kit will be in use
4. The distance from definitive medical care
5. The availability of rescue (such as access to helicopter evacuations)
6. Your medical expertise and/or the expertise of other group members
7. Pre-existing problems of group members (such as diabetes)

Evaluate and repack your first aid kit before every trip. Renew medications that have reached expiration dates. Replace items that have been damaged by heat, cold, or moisture. Consider altering the contents dependent on the environment.

Do not fill your kit with items you do not know how to use. Maintain a high level of familiarity with the proper uses of all the items in your wilderness first aid kit. All members of a group should be familiar with kit contents.

Encourage each group member to pack and carry a personal first aid kit in order to reduce the size and weight of the general (group) wilderness kit.

Remember that skill and knowledge are more valuable in an emergency than the contents of a kit.

GUIDELINES FOR FIRST AID KIT CONTENTS

PERSONAL KIT

- ❏ Adhesive bandages (6)
- ❏ Sterile gauze pads, 3-by-3-inch (2)
- ❏ Adhesive tape (1 small roll)
- ❏ Moleskin, 3-by-6-inch (1)
- ❏ Soap (1 small bar) or alcohol-based hand sanitizing gel (1 travel-size bottle)
- ❏ Bacitracin ointment (1 small tube)
- ❏ Scissors (1 pair)
- ❏ Non-latex disposable gloves (1 pair)
- ❏ CPR breathing barrier (1)
- ❏ Tweezers (1 pair)
- ❏ Pencil and incident report forms

GROUP KIT

- ❏ Curlex/Kling (or equivalent), 3-inch rolls (2)
- ❏ Coban self-adhesive bandage, 2-inch roll (1)
- ❏ Adhesive tape, 1-inch rolls (2)
- ❏ Alcohol pads (12)
- ❏ Betadine pads (12)
- ❏ Assorted adhesive bandages (1 box)
- ❏ Elastic bandages, 3-inch-wide (2)
- ❏ Sterile gauze pads 4-by-4-inch (12)
- ❏ Moleskin, 3-by-6-inch (4)
- ❏ Gel pads for blister and burns (2 packets)
- ❏ Bacitracin ointment (1 tube)
- ❏ Hydrocortisone cream, 1 percent (1 tube)
- ❏ Triangular bandages (4)
- ❏ Soap (1 small bar) or alcohol-based hand sanitizing gel (1 travel-size bottle)
- ❏ Scissors (1 pair)
- ❏ Tweezers (1 pair)
- ❏ Safety pins (12)
- ❏ Non-latex disposable gloves (6 pairs)
- ❏ Protective goggles/safety glasses (1 pair)
- ❏ CPR breathing barrier (1)
- ❏ Pencil and paper
- ❏ Optional items
    - ❏ Instant cold compress
    - ❏ Space blanket
- ❏ Original size SAM Splint

ABOUT THE AUTHOR

Buck Tilton, MS, WEMT, has more than 30 years of experience in outdoor health and safety. Known and respected worldwide, he has spent most of his adult life instructing outdoor enthusiasts in wilderness medicine. He is cofounder of the Wilderness Medicine Institute of the National Outdoor Leadership School (NOLS) in Lander, Wyoming. He has written more than 1,000 magazine articles and authored or coauthored more than three dozen FalconGuides, including *Wilderness First Responder, Medicine for the Backcountry,* and *Basic Essentials of Rescue in the Backcountry.* In addition to his many writing and teaching responsibilities, Buck served on the task force that created the Boy Scouts of America Wilderness First Aid Curriculum and Doctrine Guidelines. He lives in Lander with his wife, Kat, his son, Zachary, and his daughter, BaoXin Cheyenne.

On my honor, I will do my best . . to prepare great camp food!

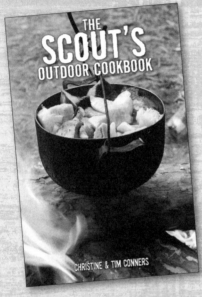

$19.95 US | $24.95 CAN
978-0-7627-4067-3
Paperback
6x9 | 408 pp

BSA item number 3453

Campout cooking is about providing sustenance, teaching thoughtfulness a
cooperation, and being grateful—not to mention healthy eating balanced
a little bit of indulgence.

This collection of recipes and tips from scouts and scout leaders represen
nearly every state in the Union celebrates the best in campout cooking.

Each recipe has been personally tested and approved by the authors and
accompanied by at-a-glance information about cooking method, challenge
level, and servings.